THE NEW LEGACY

THE
NEW LEGACY

One Texan's Thoughts on
Politics, Family, and Power

TIEMAN H. DIPPEL, JR.

TAYLOR PUBLISHING COMPANY
Dallas, Texas

Published by Taylor Publishing Company
1550 West Mockingbird Lane, Dallas, Texas 75235

Library of Congress Cataloging in Publication Data

Dippel, Tieman.
　The new legacy.

　1. Texas—Politics and government—1951–　.　2. Texas—Economic
conditions.　3. Mass media—Texas.　4. Family—Texas.　5. Power (Social
sciences)　I. Title.
JK4816.D56　　　1987　　　976.4′063　　　87-24351
ISBN 0-87833-528-5

Printed in the United States of America

9 8 7 6 5 4 3 2 1

CONTENTS

ACKNOWLEDGMENTS

I owe an inestimable debt of gratitude to many friends and associates who helped research, draft and edit this book. Chief among these are Robyn and George Pond. Their unquestioned commitment throughout the work—with letters, tapes, revisions and rewrites—showed great dedication to the ideas expressed throughout this book. Their countless hours over several years was joined by the efforts of family, friends, patient editors and thoughtful mentors. Each deserves mention personally—however, the one factor they share in common is a sincere concern for the common good.

FOREWORD

The New Legacy is a book about survival. It contains timeless truths and principles that the western world, to its detriment, is turning its back on today. It will be difficult for any to denounce this work because it is a desperately needed search for perspective. Dippel has history's many examples on his side, he is intelligent and learned, and he addresses his readers with urgency and concern.

Former Governor Allan Shivers about a year before he died remarked: "Dippel represents the desire for cohesive leadership versus the divided approach. He believes that sincerity and truthfulness outweigh deceit and misrepresentation. . . ." Former Governor John Connally has called Dippel a "young man of vision" who has proven his commitment to every sector of our society. Respect is one constant word one hears when Dippel's name is mentioned; friend and foe alike acknowledge his integrity.

Through the years, Dippel (40) has tended to his duties as CEO of the consistently profitable Brenham National Bank while actively taking up countless causes. Asked why he remains in small-town Brenham instead of selling the family business and moving to a major city in the state, Dippel quotes the answer his father gave to him: "Brenham still holds the values that first brought your great grandfather to this state almost 100 years ago. Some of these values will change, but most will remain the same as they have throughout history. . . ."

Dippel's father was trying to leave his son a legacy of traditional values. Dippel recounts the instructions he had from his father—the principles he hopes to live by today. At this momentous time in history, it's those values and principles that give Dippel clear insight and vision to peel away illusion and reveal reality on issues that beset Texas and the western world.

It's the old legacy that in truth has become the new legacy, and if Dippel is right, it is the only one, eternal legacy that we should leave to our children. Dippel believes that Texans have to change their behavior just as much as the rest of the population of the United States if they are to have a more glorious future than past. Dippel warns us that America is on a downward slide similar to that of other nations in history; just because we live here doesn't mean it won't happen and that we can remain complacent. Evidence, Dippel asserts, is all around that we are in decline—be it the breakdown of our families, our budget deficit, trade deficit, lack of confidence in our leaders, sleazy business practices, downright laziness, protectionism, sexual permissiveness, and forsaking individual responsibility. On top of which there is no overall agreement on what we stand for as a nation. Is it any wonder our young are cynical? There is confusion and indifference everywhere. "Live now—pay later" seems to be the general attitude, and Dippel warns that payday is just around the corner.

The only hope lies in drastic change and staunchly seeking sound economic values and principles, as well as developing citizens who take pride in individual responsibility. Dippel asks us to pause and contemplate what it was that made the United States of America a most noble and freedom loving country. Especially, he says, we must ask why Texas is losing its reputation as the last outpost of people who once clung to the traditional values of self-discipline, character, and courage. We should never lose sight of what really made Texas a truly great state. It's not the state's size, although that is impressive, or its mineral wealth, which is world-renowned, or its agricultural output which supplies food stuffs in massive abundance. Our greatest resource, our most magnificent product has always been our people.

Dippel reckons that if Texas fails to reach its potential, it will in large part be due to the popular notion that to take the struggle out of our existence, to make life easy, is to make life good. Neglecting to realize that it is the struggle in life that creates character, and it's character in people that builds excellence, and it's that excellence that produces a truly honored state or nation.

Individual greatness, statewide greatness, and national greatness all stem from the same thing: the will to confront adversity and overcome it. We must ask ourselves if the current generation of Texans will react to adversity as well as those who preceded us.

Dippel assures Texans that if they confront problems with integrity, ethics, and responsibility as stewards of the future, the state will overcome its present grave situation. History is against this happening, but if it does occur, Dippel's book, *The New Legacy* will be recorded as a significant contribution made at the eleventh hour.

Jack Martin
Publisher
Texas Business Magazine

PREFACE

Each of us at certain times in our lives sense our own mortality. It usually occurs in those instances that we search for ways to find and fulfill our most personal goals. Some people pursue the honors of worldly acclaim, others seek a sense of honor which comes from having a satisfied conscience, and others aspire to deep spiritual peace.

As I began writing this book in my 40th year of life, it was a time of reflection about those years during which I gathered information about the world and tried to follow the steps that would lead to a successful life. During those 40 years, the knowledge and pace of the world have expanded immensely from the period of my early youth in a small Texas town. I can remember vividly how uncomplicated life seemed and how I hoped to be old enough to see the many sights of the world and to play an active part in it. In those 40 years, fate has provided me a grand opportunity to see and participate in many things. I've seen how our traditional wisdom, with which we try to deal with life's rapid changes, is often overburdened by technology's compounded growth. The Texas, and indeed, the America of the past are gone forever in the historical sense of economics, politics, and our approach to communications and culture. The economics of the world is now international; politics centers on new and different issues and even media's news coverage becomes ever more superficial in order to include all that needs to be shown.

The family that has been the nucleus of our society has seen equally dramatic change. As my children reached the age of understanding, I struggled to teach them how the world works and life's significance with the same type of simplicity and logic that my father had used with me. He felt every man could make a difference and had a responsibility in life. His values were those that came from the Texas frontier. They were based on a strong belief in the importance of ideas such as liberty and freedom of religion and an appreciation of moral principles which spring from belief in God. To explain how the world works to children, you have to communicate through their perspective. Every person is different because of his experiences, background and level of awareness on various issues. The best that I felt I could do for my children was to try to give them a perspective of how I saw the world and teach them the importance of thinking on their own because life is ever-changing, and the most important values they could learn were the importance of commitment to their beliefs and the knowledge that they were responsible for using their talents to the highest ends possible.

When I started writing this book I had intended to deal with the philosophies of Machiavelli, Aristotle, and the precepts of many other major thinkers and artists of eastern and western civilization. I wanted to urge people to rally behind statesmanship as a wiser approach to problem-solving, as opposed to political maneuvers based on special interests. But as the work progressed, it became clear that statesmanship requires public support. For politicians to risk being statesmen, they must have backing by constituents who are exercising a higher vision of informed and responsible citizenship.

To effectively grapple with the enormity of the subject would have required that *The New Legacy* be issued in volumes on a monthly basis. The history of ideas and philosophies, the art of political strategy, or the importance of the arts are fit topics for books in themselves.

I realized that my perspective of the world is a product of the heritage of America, Texas, and most intimately, Brenham. My foundation was built carefully, as no doubt yours was, by a father and mother who faithfully passed along family tradition and culture. Although I have been privileged to meet thinkers throughout the United States and other parts of the world, and they have enriched my understanding, the basic elements of my personal philosophy remain rooted in the soil of Brenham. I think it's safe to say that your understanding of the world is likewise based upon your childhood and familial relationships. My hope is that you will see similarities between my experiences in Brenham and your experiences wherever you were raised. I hope you will be encouraged to think about your own set of perspectives, to review the origins of those ideas which have created your personal world and to analyze consciously the concepts and values that affect you today and may lead you along new pathways in the future.

This book represents a sharing of my understanding about dealing effectively in the arenas of communication, economic, and political power. I write from my heart and my small-town Texas heritage. This is not meant to be a "how to" treatise. It is one man's perspective from a certain point in time. It presents ideas and observations, but doesn't presume to give final answers. I hope it will convey some basic information regarding certain critical topics and their interrelationships that may bring about a greater awareness of how the world works and can be affected. If this book alerts you, provides deeper insight, or motivates you to further study, then it will have served a useful purpose.

Although few people can change the course of history, we each have influence in our own time and place. This book is my affirmation that it is not naive to hold onto certain traditional values and principles. We are, in effect, only a generation removed from the cave men if we do not pass onto our children what we know. We need to help them learn about the world and life in its fullest, broadest, and most integrated perspective. There is genius in specialized comprehension of one subject, but true genius lies in the appreciation of multiple, related ideas and the practical application of that knowledge. I believe that we enjoy life more if we discover its purpose. This requires deepening our awareness and assuming individual responsibility. When our lives on earth are finished, many of us want to be able to look back and know that we have influenced and helped others in some way. This book is written in support of that legacy.

Tieman Dippel
July, 1987

THE NEW LEGACY

One Father's Words

"Now, I don't want you to worry about me. I will get over this as I have survived everything else. But just in case something unexpected should happen to me, I want you to take charge. Don't let the family dwell upon it. Time and life go on. I have been fortunate to be able to live my life as a lion. Two weeks of that is worth a lifetime as a lamb.

"I chose to keep our family in Brenham and Texas, rather than going to other places and trying new opportunities. That might have been more profitable, but Brenham still holds the values that first brought your great-grandfather to this state almost 100 years ago. Some of these values will change, but most will remain the same as they have throughout history. It is important to remember that no matter how they try in Congress, they cannot repeal the law of gravity. God's laws and natural laws are the ultimate power in this world. Some people may only discover them after a lifetime, but they do exist. Recognizing them is critical.

"The most important thing I can leave you is a good name, and I think I have done that. Your mother and I have worked and saved a long time to create this beginning for you and your sister. Home has always been the most important part of our lives and should be of yours. We hope we have taught you the importance of our values and passed along our heritage. You have an education that will help you achieve what is really important in life—being a responsible citizen, loving husband, and sensitive father. There may be more to living, but these three areas can make your life deeply satisfying.

"What I feel I will be leaving you is an opportunity—a start from which you can make your own mark. The time that we spend on earth is relatively small in comparison with the great movement of history. All we can do within our life span is to make the world better than it was when we first arrived. All fortunes eventually are dispersed, but the ideas and values

1

that you leave to society can live forever. I hope you and Kitty will have a wonderful family, just as your mother and I had with you and Deanna. Being a good father is your greatest challenge and responsibility. Teach your children the ideals you think are proper. Give them the best values that you can. And teach them how to judge what is best for their lives and nation. We must try to make every generation's character better than the one before it and build a higher standard of living through wise policies.

"Don't underestimate the power and value of ideas, politics, and money. But never let any of these be your God. Learn to acquire and use them, but make absolutely certain that you understand the purposes for which they are being used.

"Lots of things have changed in Texas since I was a young man, and they will continue to change even faster during the next 20 years as your generation assumes leadership. You will need to keep a clear sense of what's important. I remember hearing how my dad came to Texas from Germany. Whenever a family suffered a bad harvest or business disaster, their neighbors helped them out until they were able to get back on their feet again. Now it seems that everyone is out for his own piece of the pie regardless of who else starves. There is still charity, but people are sometimes too busy to hear their consciences. Too often even charity itself is commercialized; but if a dime out of each dollar reaches the needy, it is worth our efforts.

"Life is already different from a few years ago. I'm worried about the way politics is changing. People don't know their leaders personally. They don't seem to have the same respect as they did in my day for the ideas that made America strong. Texas can have great impact on our country. But as Texans, we can either mature and bring our ideas to other Americans, or we can create a petty state that will be defeated by partisanship. If that happens, we will make little difference.

"I have hope that you and other young people can understand the changes occurring in politics and economics and how they affect you. Then you'll be able to handle them. In the process, you'll turn Texas and America in a more positive direction again.

"Remember to associate with people who care more about whether they go to heaven or hell than whether they become governor of Texas or head of a company. Ambition can be your worst enemy. Often you are not a good leader until you have lost your ambition and come face to face with what is most important in life. Guard against both ambition and pride, or in the long run you will be a loser, perhaps not in appearance, but in reality. You will have to deal with all types of people in life. Some will be genuine and others not. It will be hard to judge them until you have had experience with

them. Do not hesitate to cultivate friendships because that is what makes life enjoyable. However, watch new acquaintances for awhile before giving them your trust.

"One certainty in life is that you are not always on top. There are many people who try to avoid the falls by changing philosophies. These are people of convenience. They're often successful in the short term, while they are on earth. But I have always wondered whether they were successful in the sense of eternity. I feel following conscience is a far better guide.

"Remember to judge people on their merit and not by their possessions or jobs. People should be judged by how they use their success rather than by how much they acquire. There is a difference between self-respect and pride. Just as there always will be differences in abilities and destinies, there always will be economic distinctions. But we have a responsibility to allow people to keep their self-respect. Your grandfather taught this to me early in life when he took me to his wholesale grocery. The Depression made life in Texas very tough, and few people made money. Everyone helped his neighbors and enjoyed closeness and cooperation. Your grandfather and I would slit open sacks of flour and spend what seemed to be a lifetime trying to crack, not break, some eggs. I thought this was one of the most foolish things I had ever seen and could not understand why he would ruin good merchandise at a time when everyone was losing money.

"So he sat down with me, and we had a conversation I always will remember. He said his employees had helped him build the business. They had gone through many hard years together to make the business a success. They all knew he couldn't afford to keep them on, but my dad felt he had a responsibility to help. Dad said, 'If you offer these people money for doing nothing, some of them would not take it because they would lose their self-respect. Those who would accept the money would suffer equally from a loss of inner strength.' So, I watched with admiration as my father offered damaged goods to his former employees in exchange for helping help him move the merchandise.

"The older you become, the more you'll recognize the importance of finding a purpose in life. But first you need to learn about reality. Emotion more than thought rules your life when you are a child. Ambition and ego guide your conscience more than responsibility. As your maturity and understanding develop, you'll think about mortality. Your thoughts will reach a deeper level of understanding. You will discover that God gave you freedom of choice in how you live your life. The most important thing you can do is to find a sense of love and oneness with God and other people. I became a better person when I learned the lessons of stewardship and how to

deal with others by reading the Bible. In that way, I found my own meaning for life. You will go through a similar process as you question why you were put on this earth.

"The rule of the world is not just to take from life, but to put something back. We all have responsibilities, although sometimes we would like to ignore them, especially the difficult ones. Some men can affect very little, but they still have the responsibility to do what they can in a positive way. I have tried to do that. On occasions I have been right, and on others I've been wrong. When I was wrong, I was able to admit it. At least God knew my motives. That makes the later times of life, like these, a lot more satisfying.

"There are many things you can learn from the Bible. The parable of the talents teaches you that all of us are judged by what we do with our resources. The more ability you are given, the more is expected of you. God has given you a number of abilities. Please don't waste them."

·   ·   ·

It was hard to accept that my father was dying.

"If a man is fortunate he will, before he dies, gather up as much as he can of his civilized heritage and transmit it to his children. And to his final breath he will be grateful for this inexhaustible legacy, knowing that it is our nourishing mother and our lasting life."

—WILL AND ARIEL DURANT

I.

PASSING THE TORCH

Dad was a man who had always recovered from misfortune. Yet when my wife, Kitty, and I returned home in 1971 on Christmas leave from the Navy, I could see that his heart condition and emphysema were taking a heavy toll. Dad had been in St. Luke's Hospital in Houston during Thanksgiving, and he had wanted desperately to come home to Brenham to be with the whole family. Perhaps he sensed it would be his last Christmas with us.

I sat next to Dad in silence. The bedroom looked the same as it had during my childhood in the 1950s. The high, sturdy oak bed was covered with a handmade quilt that was something of a family heirloom. Many times in my youth I would tiptoe into Mother and Dad's room in the middle of the night and climb under that quilt, when the world was too cold or the nightmares too frighteningly real. That quilt, rumpled and worn by years of use, was a cherished part of the family. It was like some of the tools Dad had kept from his youth. He could have replaced them, but he believed that getting rid of those old tools or throwing out that quilt would have the same effect on us children as the death of our faithful dog, Blackie. They were symbols of our family's closeness—symbols that created an atmosphere that tied us together. Perhaps these things had no monetary value, but they were priceless in terms of emotion because they could bring back instantly the remembrances of a lifetime.

5

Family pictures jockeyed for position on the dresser top. Smiling faces told of time passing—a happy courtship, years of war and service. Snapshots of two children were tucked in the frame of the large wedding photo. The cedar chest held linens embroidered by family and friends, and the wood-encased Singer sewing machine stood silently in the corner where it had served active duty when my younger sister, Deanna, and I were growing up.

Someone knocked at the front door. I heard Mother graciously accept the fruit cake as she asked the guest to stay and visit. It was then that I realized why Christmas was so important to Dad. It symbolized what life was about—closeness, family, friends . . . taking time to do what was *important*.

When we were young, Deanna and I would race each other home from school during the holidays to see what special foods had arrived or would emerge from the oven—or better yet, what new packages were under the tree. Dad specialized in pancakes, and there was always a gallon of maple syrup, a gift from a special friend at Christmas. Cookies in the form of gingerbread men and "Santa Claus faces" warmed our afternoons. We remained curious about the taste of the rum balls, but they were off-limits. (We were told that only Santa ate those, during his mysterious visit on Christmas Eve.)

In later years Christmas became the main time our family was together, and our celebrations took on a rarer quality than ever before. To Dad, in particular, Christmas had a special significance because it symbolized the meaning of being a family.

The room hadn't changed during the years I was at the University of Texas and then in the Navy. It was Dad who had changed. The pictures remained, but time wasn't waiting. Nor was it waiting for Brenham. Sitting in Dad's room, I thought about our safe and secure home and the town that always had been part of my life. The St. Anthony Hotel and the post office sat at one end of Main Street in Brenham, with the Simon Movie Theatre and the railroad tracks at the other. The jailhouse was built of stone and stood near the post office at the end of Alamo Street. All the kids imagined that it was filled with outlaws who had to be carefully housed until their fate would be decided on the third floor of the courthouse.

During his 20 years as Sheriff of Washington County, Dad started a tradition of taking various groups of older boys through the jail where he always seemed to have at least one prisoner in a cell. He would tell the boys that this was the "Wild Man of Green Mountain," whom he had just captured. He'd impress upon them that the fellow was one of the most dangerous criminals ever held captive in Brenham. The prisoner would rattle the bars, scream, and absolutely terrify most of the kids. Then the jailer would call Dad to go downstairs. He'd tell the boys that he'd be back in just a minute and then close the door. Just after he left, the wild man would come over to the cell door, push on it, and shockingly, it would open. They would trip over each other heading for the door, which was locked. The wild man would growl and move toward them. Then he would stop and say, "This is a bad place you want to stay away from." About that time, Dad would return, and he and the "trustee" would explain the difference between the bright and dark sides of life. Later he told me he never had to lock up any of the kids who had taken that tour.

And, of course, there was Citizens' Pharmacy, which had the best soda fountain in the area and was famous for its super-thick chocolate malts. It was a popular place to meet your friends, and our local dentist handed out certificates that entitled the bearers to special sundaes at the pharmacy. (The certificates were awarded to those who didn't move in the chair, cry, or bite Dr. Stafford's finger.)

There were a number of cafes, including Otto's, Schoenemann's, and Kean's, where the men gathered each morning to catch up on the news from yesterday, debate politics, and discuss the future of cattle and crops. The lawyers, bankers, and merchants would visit regularly, whereas the farmers would drop by only on special occasions and weekends. In the old days, the townspeople would visit each merchant and pay their bills in cash on Friday afternoons. As that practice declined, breakfast at a local coffee shop served as the information channel. The area's economy was dominated by ranching, cotton farming in the Brazos Bottom, and a little oil production. Like the rest of Texas, the land and people were inextricably tied together which gave the area a true rural character and preserved frontier values.

As we grew older, we realized Brenham was surrounded by a much larger Texas than what we knew as children. Powerful, bold Houston sat about 65 miles east of us. Dripping with oil and money, it was a brash town that beckoned teenage boys who devised ways of sneaking off on Friday nights without the folks finding out. The older boys would hang out at the local Dairy Queen for a while until they found others daring enough to attempt the escape to Houston. Those of us slightly younger and far more timid would watch with hidden admiration. Later in the '60s, rock concerts came to Houston. For years, we country boys (and of course our parents) thought Houston was synonymous with pandemonium and danger.

More tranquil and subdued Washington-on-the Brazos was about twenty miles northeast of town. Lots of families picnicked there at the state park. This was the birthplace of the Republic of Texas in 1836, and the town had served as the Republic's first capital. Texas' current capital, Austin, was about an hour and a half drive west from Brenham. Most people never considered traveling that far unless they were visiting sons and daughters at the University of Texas or were involved in state politics. The rival state university, Texas A & M, was about thirty-five miles north of Brenham in College Station. By standing on Gindorf's Bluff overlooking the Brazos River, you could see College Station and the green fields of young cotton stretching endlessly along the river valley.

The Gindorfs lived in one of the area's early plantation homes. Dad and I visited Mr. Gindorf every now and then, and he'd tell us about early Texas history and the Brazos River below. Legend had it that Sam Houston, when he lived in nearby Independence, camped on what was then called Hidalgo Bluff to contemplate Texas' future. William Barrett Travis, who died at the Alamo, had a ranch at Chappell Hill just to the southeast, and Stephen F. Austin had his ranch to the south at San Felipe. Dad and Mr. Gindorf also talked of old friends, long forgotten by most, who had contributed so much to shape this area by building roads and cotton mills and providing leadership for the community. They had emerged not so much for what they owned, but for what they had done to help others.

Mother walked in with Dad's medicine and fixed the bedsheets. She had begun her role as a nurturer at age 16 when she lost her own mother to cancer, only a year after her father had died from a heart attack at 42. Mother always felt this was related to the pneumonia he contracted in France in World War I. As the oldest of three children, she assumed much of the responsibility for her brothers, Scott and Kinch. Life was difficult. There was little time to enjoy being young since shortly thereafter she also became the administrator of a local hospital. Like Dad, she had wanted to continue her education, but the Depression and family responsibilities forced them both to cut their schooling short. They drew great strength and satisfaction, however, from the closeness of their families, as they overcame one problem after another. I think that was why they insisted that Deanna and I get as full an education as possible. And Mother often reminded us that we should *never* stop learning.

I remember when Mother was taking sewing lessons in the old stone courthouse, which stood in the middle of Brenham's town square. Dad told Deanna and me to stay right by the courthouse, while he visited with a man who sought him on a matter for the Sheriff's office. While we were playing, Deanna accidentally fell, hitting her face squarely on the stone steps. I ran to her, and together we looked at the little white piece of tooth she held in her palm. Deanna screamed, which summoned Dad and Mother to the scene almost simultaneously. I don't think Mother ever fully recovered from the incident; she blamed herself for taking that sewing lesson, rather than being with us. Somehow, she thought if only she had been there, the accident would not have happened. Her life centered on our family to the exclusion of almost everything else. I wondered uneasily how she would handle Dad's death.

As Washington County Sheriff and then later president of Farmers National Bank for fourteen years, Dad had been for me a bulwark of strength and a symbol of what was good and right in Texas. I'll always remember him eating breakfast with us every morning before he left for work—dressed in his sheriff's uniform with neatly creased brown pants, starched khaki shirt, and a shining, polished badge pinned over his right-hand shirt pocket. He'd talk to Mom about the usual things—chores to be done, upcoming town events, or friends he had seen the day before. Sometimes he'd tell a story about some lawbreaker who had to be locked up after a midnight brawl in the city lounge. My cereal would turn soggy as I listened. My eyes must have opened like saucers, because Dad would stop in the middle of his tale, look at me, and start to chuckle. Mom would clear her throat, and all of a sudden the story would come to a stop.

Mother was a cultured and refined woman. She came from a successful family of highly respected physicians, nurses, and prominent leaders with roots in Scandinavia, Germany, England, and Texas. Mother tried to teach us the values of a civilized life, good manners and etiquette. Dad always said he sprang from the entrepreneurial side of Texas since his father had started both the Brenham Wholesale Company and the Dippel Coffee Company that originated the Old Homestead Brand. He used to kid me that if I looked too far, I might find more horse thieves than ministers in his family tree. Even though that wasn't the case, ancestral lineage didn't interest him. Individual merit did. His point was simple—every man makes his own life and has his own virtues. Inherited money might create power; social prominence might command respect; but in the end, what a man did on his own was what mattered, because that was all he could control.

After running the Dippel Coffee Company for a while, Dad became convinced that his future was in public service, and he decided to run for sheriff. Against several opponents, he won a majority. At that time, the sheriff's position was one of the better-paying jobs in the area. The salary was only $3,500 a year, but Texas was still recovering from the Depression and any job paying that well was important. I can recall visiting the state prison and Dad warning me that the prisoners might boo—as they had before—when his name was announced over the loudspeaker. So he was well-known at Huntsville, though not appreciated.

Dad also helped prepare cases for the district attorney. When these cases were tried, few were lost. Washington County earned a reputation as a "hanging county" with tough sentences for offenders. There was very little crime. In one case involving a dog theft, however, the state obtained an indictment, but no conviction. A young girl from a poor family had been given a registered dog by her grandmother. She had very little else in the world. When the dog disappeared, the child cried for three days and refused to eat. Dad was certain he knew who had stolen the dog in order to sell it in Houston. To him, this particular crime was worse than many others. And even though he couldn't get a final conviction, Dad took satisfaction in making the suspect face the little girl in court. He felt justice had been served in at least a small way.

In those days the office of sheriff was an important focal point in the strong Democratic network in rural Texas. If a candidate didn't have a solid base of support in the rural areas, he had little chance of getting elected. Dad used to give barbecues for peace officers from the surrounding counties as well as from other parts of the state. He would bring in the Texas Rangers, officials from the Department of Public Safety in Austin, and sheriffs from Houston, Austin, and other major cities. The main purpose of these gatherings was to get people acquainted with each other so they could exchange information on law enforcement, thereby building stronger working relationships as each officer returned to his own jurisdiction.

There was another important reason for bringing people together. These occasions helped cement political friendships which formed a solid network for winning elections at all levels of government. Dad taught several rural sheriffs the importance of having a "special deputy" in every precinct. The deputy thus had a feeling of personal investment in a sheriff's re-election, since his own badge depended on who was in office. This created a powerful political network in central Texas through which information passed and opinions were formed.

Dad knew almost all the important leaders personally, which gave him a broadened perspective about the nature of politics in the state. He maintained that it was important to learn from the most experienced and knowledgeable people in politics, business, and academics. "You are often only as good as your teachers, Skipper," Dad said. "You've got to recognize men's assets and liabilities. Learn how they acquired their strengths. Avoid their weaknesses. Certain people are much stronger than others. You will discover this as you work with them. Listen to the experience of your elders, but don't forget that times change, and you have to change with them."

Dad had three particular friends who made lasting contributions to Texas. He told me many times how he respected these men, and I remember thinking that if Dad, who was a hero to me, honored them, then I should too. Governor Allen Shivers was one. Dad liked to spend time with Deanna and me after church, and on these Sunday afternoons he often told us about the people who had done so much for our state. "Governor Shivers is a master of strategy," Dad would say. Dad believed Shivers had a commanding overview of where Texas was and where it should go. He was a courageous man who never hesitated in pushing those goals in the state senate, where he once had served as lieutenant governor. "The Governor," Dad stated, "always is aware of exactly where he wants to go, and what he wants to see accomplished. He works continually toward those ends. Somehow he knows where 51 percent of all the votes are or knows where to get them when he needs them. I really admire that in a man." Dad drew a distinction between his respect for a man's ability and power versus the admiration he had for his motives.

Dad used to say that Governor John Connally had a sense of presence—his demeanor was strong and self-confident, yet he was also kind and humble. Dad thought that Governor Connally was one of the most sincere men he had ever known, and that this sincerity came through when he spoke. In Dad's perspective, the ability to deliver a powerful speech enabled statesmen to lead people through a maze of ideas and issues. Many politicians can strong-arm in a back room, he said, but the difference between force and inspiration is the difference between darkness and light.

Governor Connally was conservative. Yet he showed initiative in such areas as education and made certain that social programs were implemented. He moved forward in such a way that people followed with a willingness to sacrifice because they believed he was going in the right direction. Dad noted that many leaders try to push people rather than lead them. "That's like trying to move a wet piece of spaghetti," he said. "If you push on it, it buckles. But if you pull from the top, it follows where you want it to go."

During a portion of Allen Shivers' term as governor, John Ben Shepherd served as attorney general. He and Dad had become friends during World War II. Dad often said that Shepherd was the state's organizational genius, having formed countless associations and commissions for the betterment of Texas. There was no doubt in my father's mind that the General would spend the rest of his life in pursuit of these same objectives because of his devotion to a unique set of values. And importantly, most of these organizations would continue to function effectively after his death. His would be a legacy of good works. General Shepherd never asked for public acclaim. On the contrary, he sought to involve more people in projects so that tasks could be accomplished apart from concerns about who received credit.

To me, Dad was like John Wayne. Both men had a sense of fairness and justice that kept order in life. Like the legendary film hero, Dad seem indestructible. But unlike John Wayne, Dad seldom carried a gun, although he had a fine, hand-tooled leather holster and a collection of pistols and rifles. Instead of guns, Dad used a long ten-cell flashlight that he had special-ordered. Whenever some fellow became belligerent and drew a knife or used fists, Dad grabbed him with one hand and hit him over the head with the flashlight with the other. He said that was one way to stun someone without inflicting serious injuries.

This technique evolved out of an encounter that took place shortly after World War II. Dad was responding to a call about trouble at one of the country dance halls. He strode through the entrance and found himself chest-to-chest with a visiting army sergeant who weighed more than 300 pounds. The sergeant was drunk and spoiling for a fight. He had already assaulted a number of local people. But Dad, with military training in the martial arts, was confident he could take charge of the situation and subdue the sergeant, thus assuring that his reputation alone would be enough to stop fisticuffs in the future.

It was a good strategy—until the soldier hauled back and swung. Dad ducked and then hit him in the skull as hard as he could with his right fist. After that punch, Dad was in trouble. It took 20 bruising minutes to get the man primarily kicked into submission. Later Dad swore he could have made more impression on a brick wall. He wasn't surprised to find that his wrist was broken. From that point forward, whether he knew martial arts or not, he believed that carrying a ten-cell flashlight was a whole lot smarter than copying John Wayne's style. He would point to the scars on his knuckles and say, "You know, for all my trying, I just seemed to end up cutting my hands on somebody's teeth." Far from finding it glamorous, Dad was convinced that violence never accomplished anything. Once a friend remarked, "It will all change when the pushing and shoving starts." Dad's response was, "Smart men are gone, if they can be, when it reaches that stage." He always noted that "karate doesn't stop bullets." Being smart enough to control the environment was far better strategy than relying on physical ability. The strong normally beat the weak, but the smart normally dominated the strong.

Dad always felt you should start with reason—violence was the other end of the spectrum. He was a devoted Christian because he had found that to be the best way to live. When people questioned how he could be such a devout believer—on one hand building churches with loans at cost, while on the other using force that might put a man in the hospital—he would simply say that churches build a community, but that it was his duty to eradicate evil. Dad had a sign in his office that read, "I don't discriminate. If you come looking for help, I'll give you all I can. If you come looking for trouble, I'll do the same." He believed in a philosophy of hating the sin, but loving the sinner. But for him, as for me, the toughest question with which he always wrestled, as I have, was, "Where is the line between Christian forgiveness and action against evil?" To Dad, it became a case of whether it was personal or a matter of principle that would affect others. It was an issue he pondered continually.

When Dad had time off we'd go to the country with our rabbit-hunting beagles. He liked hunting and wanted me to experience the same enjoyment, recognizing that this was a form of recreation which most of my generation would never fully appreciate. We hiked to an area filled with oak, pecan, and cedar trees right along the Brazos River. When I was young, there were enough rabbits for hunting. Later Dad had to import them and do everything possible to preserve them for that purpose. Sitting on an old fallen oak tree, Dad told me how I could learn a lot about dealing with people by observing nature. "You can just about anticipate a rabbit's action if you know what kind of rabbit it is," he said. "Jackrabbits tend to run and don't like water. Cottontails are inclined to duck and hide. Swamp rabbits run in a broad circle leading away from the burrow and then gradually come back to it. If you watch how the dogs are running, you can tell what kind of rabbit it is and anticipate where to position yourself to have a clean shot. It's not so different with people. Watch their actions, and they will give you a powerful indication of what they are probably going to do. People have a style, too. You learn to appreciate folks who are honest about little things. Watch out for the ones who drive up in Cadillacs with slick tires or have holes in expensive alligator boots."

In the silence of his bedroom, Dad turned to look at me. He smiled. Maybe he had been thinking about our hunting trips, too. I returned his smile and remembered how he would tell me his river story on almost every single hunt. There were lots of creeks that flowed through the gently rolling Texas hills, and one in particular, New Year's Creek, was a favorite spot of ours. We would sit on the bank to enjoy the cheese, crackers and Cokes we bought at the country store. After finishing mine,

I'd climb the rocks lining the creek and watch the minnows flit back and forth between the stones on the bottom. Sometimes bits of twigs would come floating by and the minnows would dart out of the way. Those twigs probably looked like huge logs to the minnows, just as trees looked gigantic to me as a child.

Dad would tell me how the river changes but always stays the same. Obviously, the point was very important because he told the story again and again, unconcerned about repeating himself. At first, it was like an old joke, but after a while the emphasis of the story, combined with the respect I held for Dad, took on special significance as I learned how true it was. Just as Dad told me while we sat by the creek, life changed but it remained the same. The water that flowed past the rocks and trees yesterday was now gone, but the scene was the same: One needed only to note what changed and what did not. Technology was advancing rapidly with numerous significant achievements, yet human nature had changed very little. We still witnessed greed, jealousy, and other negative emotions that could cause great problems and sorrow. I think by telling me that same story over and over, Dad was also saying that the values of honesty, hard work, and virtuous living have withstood the test of time and would help us find answers for the future. There are sound reasons why traditions survive.

Mother's voice broke the silence when she asked if I wanted lunch. I told her I would wait for Dad to go to sleep. I glanced at the wall above Mother's dresser and saw an old newspaper photograph of Dad in his "Cubs" football uniform. The team was undefeated in his senior year of high school, and my father was one of Brenham High School's outstanding football players. Some old-timers still talk about how "Jackrabbit Dippel" ran back a kickoff for the winning touchdown in the final game of a successful season.

I remember the time when a neighbor was visiting one Friday evening, and Dad first told the story of how he got the name "Jackrabbit Dippel." As a boy, Dad used to take all the neighborhood dogs to hunt rabbits at the outskirts of town. The area at that time was secluded and heavily wooded, with several creeks and a swimming hole that was a favorite among the town kids. The road leading to this swimming hole crossed a small bridge. One day the dogs spotted a jackrabbit. They ran the rabbit hard for about 20 minutes with Dad following. By listening to the dogs' howls, he knew the rabbit was circling back. Since jackrabbits avoid water, Dad figured the rabbit would go to the bridge and cross there. So he ran in that direction, arriving just as the rabbit was running across the bridge. At close range he could see the animal was exhausted. The rabbit continued up the road. Dad dropped his gun and gave chase, thinking he could catch it without wasting a shell.

Just as he was closing in on the rabbit, one of the local families happened to be driving along the road in a horse-drawn buggy. Panting, Dad ran right up beside them, grabbed the rabbit by its ears, and held it high in the air to demonstrate his success. The man was astounded. He soon spread the word around town that Dad trained for football by chasing jackrabbits and was surely the fastest young man ever seen in the history of Brenham. Dad pointed to this as a good example of why one should view acclaim skeptically. He also noted that skepticism should be applied to the stories surrounding many "heroes" of the Old West and some present-day politicians as well. Media "hype" was nothing new to him. Far wiser, he said, to judge a man by solid evidence and a long track record.

I gazed at Dad; the medicine had quieted his cough. The aroma of chicken-fried steak and cream gravy reached the room. As I closed the wooden door behind me, I was conscious of the cold, smooth texture of its brass knob. It was one of those times when a simple object evokes memories and heightens awareness. Forgetting food, I walked down the hall to my own bedroom. I looked at the pictures of me in my youth which Mother had hung on the walls. Perhaps by leaving those mementos out, Mother and Dad felt as though Deanna and I weren't so far away. I remembered my first day at school and felt again the same vague twinge of uneasiness that comes from venturing into the unknown. Mother had tried her best to cheer me up, and we went together on that first trek away from the safe fortress of home.

Our school was very small with only four grades, four rooms, and four teachers. The name, "Alamo," was carved in stone above the entrance, and it looked just like the real chapel at the Alamo Mission in San Antonio, where my early heroes, Davy Crockett, William Travis, and Jim Bowie, gave their lives to free Texas. I could not help but remember the times Dad had taken us there. Walt Disney had popularized Davy Crockett, but Dad's interest as he toured the shrine focused on James Bonham, the messenger of the Alamo. The leaders of the garrison will always be remembered for their heroism. But Bonham represented true valor. He was perhaps the most courageous of all, because he was safe when he learned Fannin would not provide support for the garrison. Knowing the Alamo was doomed, he rode back to certain death to do no more than deliver a devastating message. Some men are caught in circumstances beyond their control; others have choices. Bonham chose what he considered a responsibility to loyalty and honor and rode to his death without question. For that reason, he holds a special significance for Texans who cherish the state's history.

To understand Texans, non-Texans must realize we are very close to our history. People outside the state may remember the Alamo as a battle with a sense of honor similar to the account of Leonidus at Thermopylae. There are those who argue it was not a strategic position for the Texans and that the battle was less important than the state's history makes it. But they miss the effect it has on present Texans. If you visit Europe, you will see evidences of societies that date back a thousand or more years. Events occurred over long periods of time. The history of Texas, however, began in 1836. For many years thereafter, the area remained a frontier characterized by Comanche raids on the plains, continued friction with Mexico, and constant battles with the elements. Our story is recent and vivid.

The hardships of frontier life established an enduring set of values in the people of Texas. Dad learned from his parents and grandparents who were literally a part of that frontier. The sense of history was strong. Many citizens personally knew great men who exhibited noble ideals in their way of life.

The old Alamo School had been built as a true symbol of Texas rather than an example of architectural prowess. It stood on an elevation about four feet above ground level and was bordered by huge oak and pecan trees which had old gnarled roots that pushed through the soil and made cracks in the sidewalks. Looking up into the tops of those trees made me feel as small as those minnows in the creeks that darted from the twigs swirling in the current.

Each grade, with about 25 kids enrolled, had a quadrant of the land around the building that was considered its own turf at recess and lunch. Usually the boys played cowboys, and the girls designed houses. We allowed the girls to play with the boys if they could outrun us and weren't afraid to touch worms and crickets. We didn't mingle much with the older kids except when everybody rushed to buy chocolate milk or orange drink from an old refrigerator in the hallway during recess.

As my mind returned to the room I looked in my closet and saw my old Boy Scout uniform that Mother had carefully preserved along with my merit badges and Order of the Arrow sash. Cub Scouts was a central part of my early life. We met at Tweedy Clark's house, played football in the afternoon and enjoyed all the traditional Cub Scout activities. On weekends we had one-day campouts and learned about nature.

Mother and Dad insisted that I devote myself to scouting. From

Cubs I graduated into Boy Scouts and then became an Eagle Scout. At the time, it was hard to see the value of all this work. While most of my friends were dating, I was working on merit badges. Sometimes they kidded me about not having much time for girls, and I thought that Mother and Dad were old-fashioned and unreasonable.

Finally, I asked Dad if there were not better things for me to do. Dad had been a Scoutmaster even before Deanna and I were born. He explained, "If you don't want to be second best, you've got to be willing to commit the time, effort and dedication toward being the most you can be. If you ever give up, even for an instant, you will take steps backward. Scouting teaches important values and special skills, but more than that, it forms character that becomes a part of you. Do you remember the exact moment when you learned to swim, ride a bike, or roller skate? No, they've become habits, and that's the point I'm trying to make. You don't recall learning to swim. You just get into the water, and you swim by habit. I don't remember when I learned to ride a bicycle or roller skate, but once each of those skills had been mastered, the knowledge was part of me.

"The same thing is true of dedication. If you quit when you are young or take the easy way out, then it is unlikely you will ever succeed. If you learn dedication early in life, it becomes a habit and a part of your character. You won't have to struggle constantly against laziness because the qualities of persistence, devotion, and courage will be habits. Sometimes older people are able to form good habits later in life if they recognize their shortcomings and work very hard to change. But for most adults, it is too difficult. That is why Mother and I want you to have the best possible beginning." He finished speaking and looked at me. I could see his love and concern for me reflected in his eyes and expression.

Sticking to a job, doing it as well as possible, and seeing it through to completion became easier as I got older. It became habit. Through the years I remembered that conversation with Dad. It touched upon a dilemma we all face at times. There is always an easy way, and there is a right way—in business, politics, or dealing with people in general. Seldom are these the same way.

Mother called me, and I walked past Dad's room quietly so that he wouldn't wake up. Even though it was December, it was 70 degrees outside, and Mom had the kitchen windows open. I sat down to lunch with Mother, Deanna, and her husband, Ron. Kitty and I had to leave for Florida the next day, where we were stationed with the Navy. Deanna and Ron had to return to the Army's Fort Polk in Louisiana. I don't think they realized the seriousness of Dad's condition because he kept up a convincing front in their presence, retiring to the bedroom before anyone noticed his energy was drained. We were chatting about the Christmas which had just passed, and exchanging information on our travel plans. Mother poured coffee to go along with the leftover cookies and Collin Street fruitcake, a gift from our neighbor. After the holiday preparations and celebrations, it was relaxing to sit around the table and just talk. Mother looked a little tired. It was obvious that Dad was on her mind constantly. As if to brush aside her worry and make the most of the hours left together, she briefed us on the local news and mentioned last year's Maifest.

German immigrants started the Maifest celebration, which is celebrated on Mother's Day weekend, in the 1880s. For years it was the focus of our spring activities. When I was small, I'd usually go to the Junior Maifest dressed like Roy Rogers. Other kids wore costumes representing anything from carrots and tomatoes to Dale Evans and the Lone Ranger. There was a Maifest king and queen for both the junior and senior groups. For the Senior Maifest, the high school kids dressed up in long evening dresses and tuxedos, as well as costumes for the "coronation," and went to parties held every evening. Maifest meant two solid days of parades, floats, parties, carnivals and an abundance of food. We filled our plates with traditional favorites like barbecue and kolatches until we could eat no more. School was in session, but we did very little work during that time. Relatives and neighbors who had moved away years before returned from all over the state for family reunions, giving their children the chance to participate in the festivities. There was happiness, as old friends were reunited, and sadness as we learned about the passing of special people. I thought of Dad, and I looked at Mother who was engrossed in telling Deanna about upcoming marriages and expected babies. The ongoing worry about Dad had subsided for a few moments, and they chatted happily.

Kitty and I quietly excused ourselves to drive around town to revisit the area. I still had an ominous feeling that our life would be changing, and there would be major decisions to face shortly. I told her about my thoughts while sitting with Dad and how Brenham had always been a place that seemed safe and secure while the rest of the world changed around me. After the Navy, we faced decisions about moving to Austin or Houston, where I had offers from law firms, or possibly considering business opportunities in other parts of the country, or perhaps moving back to Brenham for the values of life that it represented. I had been happier in Brenham than I was in either Law School or Naval Justice School. It wasn't a question of success. I had been successful in both business school and law school. But I was old enough to understand that happiness had to include satisfaction.

There is a Japanese saying: "To be happy is to be content." I appreciated the meaning of that. The choice between a successful family in Brenham and a political or business career with more glory elsewhere was difficult. I had seen politics at close range, understood its demands on family, and the consequent pressure and frustration. If all I accomplished was becoming well-known, I would never be content. Brenham seemed to be the right choice. The future might offer other options. Not all of us can be the quarterbacks or pitchers who directly influence the game, but we can all be players. Money was important in business, but it was far from everything. When Houstonians made enough money, the first thing they did was buy a ranch in Brenham. So Kitty and I thought we'd be one step ahead if we started there.

More importantly, our town still paid respect to the values that kept Dad there in a time when many people had packed their families and belongings and moved on. Missing that sense of place or roots, they returned. Competition in the larger world created a petty atmosphere of self-concern. Brenham had preserved a feeling of community oneness and pride that gave us warmth and security.

I didn't feel that we were settled yet. Our course was still open; our permanent home not yet established. Kitty was born and raised in Nacogdoches, Texas, home of Stephen F. Austin University. She went to Sweetbriar College in Virginia and studied in Paris before we met at the University of Texas. She had an equally strong sense of place and background. Nacogdoches is a beautiful town set among the piney woods of east Texas, and it too has an exceptional spirit of community cohesiveness.

As we drove through Brenham, Kitty reminded me of something Dad had observed. Some people are ambitious for worldly success and public honor, while others desire the confidence which comes from being part of a community where they can build a foundation of security and strength for their families. Kitty had defined our options aptly. Finding the right place—that sense of belonging—was vital for the full life a family should enjoy.

When we returned to the house, we certainly had not reached any conclusions about our lives, but we sensed a new direction, one that might lead us back to Brenham. We climbed the front steps. Mother was at the door to welcome us. Dad was still sleeping, but she was planning to wake him for dinner. I thought about Dad lying in the back bedroom—how his life was passing and mine was changing. Mother put her arm around Kitty and told her she had some things to give us for our apartment in Florida. They disappeared into the kitchen. Not wanting to disturb Dad until dinner, I sat in his oversized chair where he liked to read the books he had collected on the Old West and the Civil War. Glancing over each binding, I came across Mother's notebook on our family tree. I opened the cover slowly so that the loose newspaper clippings wouldn't fall out and turned to the material on Grandfather Dippel.

As the owner of Brenham Wholesale, he regularly drove his team of horses to all of the rural stores. Grandfather's ability to speak four languages, including Yiddish, helped considerably with the merchants and farmers who spoke only their native tongues. I thought about the Germans who settled the Texas Hill Country and built towns like Industry, where my other grandfather lived, Brenham, Fredericksburg, New Braunfels, and others. Immigrants from Sweden, Czechoslovakia, Poland, England, Ireland, Scotland, and Italy found the fertile soil of central Texas ideal for raising cattle and growing crops of all types. They brought with them a diversity of cultures and beliefs, and their children maintained and nurtured these traditions because their worth had been proven over time.

Generations of Texans have passed onto their children a respect for hard work, faith in God, persistence, independence and a love of freedom which gave them the opportunity to govern themselves. In Texas, neighbor helps neighbor, and people know what it means to cooperate.

The name Texas comes from the Tejas Indian tribe that was living in the territory when the settlers arrived. "Tejas," when translated into English, means "friendly." Because Texas was a rugged frontier, cooperation was essential. Each group of immigrants brought its own dream of opportunity and freedom. Perhaps, I thought, it was the vastness of territory or the wide open sky which spoke to their spirits and challenged them to believe in the unlimited potential of this untamed land. Whatever the call, many responded, and their fierce independence and love of freedom passed to their descendants. Habits were formed to last for generations. These basic qualities, still with us today, make Texas a unique place with an unusual character.

Mother and Kitty walked into the living room carrying assorted boxes with china, an almost new waffle iron, a toaster, and other odds and ends that thoughtful mothers-in-law give to their new daughters. The scene is etched in my memory because I wondered how in the world I was going to get anything else back to Florida. We loaded the boxes into the backseat of our blue Chevy and went back into the house to wake Dad for dinner.

He was awake, dressed and sitting in the big rocker next to the bedroom window. Once he got steady on his feet, we walked into the kitchen for dinner. Kitty and I shared some of our discussion about trying to decide what course to take after the Navy. Dad appeared pleased that we were considering moving back to Brenham to work with him at the bank. He had always wanted this, but he never tried to impose it on me. He suggested that I come by the bank before leaving for Florida. I promised to do that, and all of us moved into the living room to enjoy our few hours left together.

By the time we got up the next morning, Dad had already left for the bank. After breakfast, Kitty and I went downtown to register for absentee voting. Then she went back to the house to pack for the trip to Florida.

I left the courthouse and crossed the street to the bank. The three-story courthouse was built as a WPA project in the Depression, and the two-story marble and granite bank also belonged to that era. There was something reassuring about walking into the bank as I had done many times before. It made Dad's illness seem far away, and I could almost believe that things were as they always had been. A partition formed Dad's small corner office behind the row of teller cages. The same solid oak desk took up most of the floor space. His shotgun and rifle, which he used for his infrequent hunting trips, stood at an angle in the corner near the desk. I assumed he still had the 45-caliber gun in the right-hand desk drawer along with the Bowie knife he used for a letter opener. I often wondered if he kept them as reminders of his days as sheriff or because he intended to personally head off any bank robber. It was probably a little of both.

His desk, as always, was piled eight to ten inches deep in papers. His chair was arranged in such a way that he could talk face-to-face with customers rather than looking at them from across the desk. There was room for only one chair, and his secretary's desk was close by. Crowded conditions were a by-product of the bank's rapid growth. Dad spoke of a number of things, but his paramount concern was that I understood that I could make my life what I wanted it to be. He told me that he was hoping I would decide to make Brenham my home. He could use help, and he would teach me everything he knew about banking, and more importantly, about people. He had a lot of business contacts who could help me, but ultimately every man had to forge his own relationships, and not even he could pass them on to me.

Saying these words troubled his breathing, and he started to cough. When the spasm had subsided, he looked at me but didn't say anything.

Maybe we both were thinking the same unmentionable thought. Dad had never been a man to show his feelings, but at this moment he seemed to be choking back tears. My face turned hot, and we embraced each other tightly. Dad had always been able to keep solid control of himself, and I was not sure how to react. It was obvious that he was trying to hide any display of weakness, so I felt the best that I could do was to go on. Dad stepped back abruptly, fumbled for his wallet, and pulled out some money.

"Take Kitty out to dinner on me. Buy her a steak dinner at a nice place," he said smiling, using the same words he always did. He slapped the bill into my hand. "When you get to Florida, have fun and remember what I have taught you."

That was the last time I saw Dad.

"Train up a child in the way he should go, and when he is old he will not depart from it."

II.

FAMILY

The years since Dad's death have rushed past me. Change has brought both good times and bad. But the births of my three children produced the most significant changes in my life. As Dad had taught our family, I now was responsible for instructing my son and two daughters how to develop character, values, and the morality to guide them through the world they will inherit. Before Tee, Meg, and Buffy were born, the role of family leader and counselor seemed clear-cut. Now I think I have learned as much, if not more, about life than have my children.

For example, I learned a priceless lesson in perspective through my oldest daughter, Meg. I had spent a large amount of money landscaping our yard, and after years of effort, the project was finally completed for the Maifest. Several mornings later, I was shocked to find hundreds of toilet tissue streamers cascading from our 50-foot pecan trees. Meg had had a slumber party the night before, and the culprits were some boys her age. After viewing the scene with me, Meg exclaimed, "Oh, Dad, isn't it great! It's a real compliment."

I marched into the house to find Kitty, imagining how decorative the trees would be in winter with toilet paper still clinging to their limbs. After hearing about the prank, Kitty said, "Well, I'm glad. This builds Meg's confidence." I was afraid I couldn't share her perspective until she added, "Besides, Skipper, they could have 'egged' us."

Experiences such as that only reinforced my awareness that raising a family required greater depth of character than I had realized. I remember one evening when the kids wanted to see Halley's Comet. The four of

23

us drove into the country to Riverbend Park on the Brazos where the city lights were dimmed. Blackness engulfed us as we sat in the chill of the late evening hours trying to catch a glimpse of the comet's fuzzy tail through a telescope. As we gazed into the splendor of millions of stars, I thought about Dad. It had been years since he and I had sat together under the same sky during our hunting and fishing trips. Now as I looked upward, I felt an unsettling sense of my own mortality. Here I was—a father, and an older one at that. Now I was responsile for giving my children a view of God and the world which would sustain them and future generations. At once I felt insignificant and unequal to the task as I looked into the heavens—one lifetime seemed so short compared to the eons which stretched on either side of that moment. Yet, at the same time, our existence has immense importance because we have been created as spiritual beings with freedom of choice. Dad had thought that freedom was one of the greatest gifts given to us by our Creator. I suspect that this was the reason he loved every minute of life and tried to put every day to its highest and best use. To Dad, the important things in life were his sense of honor and his relationship to God. He often told me that regardless of a man's position or influence, the crucial question was whether he allowed his life and actions to glorify himself or glorify God.

As I sat looking at the stars with my children, I think I fully appreciated what Dad had taught us through his own life. By turning down opportunities for worldly gain in order to nurture his own household, Dad lived out his belief that a man matters little in the vastness of the universe, yet is truly important when he glorifies his Creator through his family.

To many who knew him, Dad was a study in contrasts—sensitive and concerned, but at the same time fierce and powerful. One had to understand his philosophy of hating the sin and loving the sinner to comprehend how he could be both a man of faith and a tough lawman. He taught us not to personalize issues but to recognize pettiness, jealousy, pride, and envy for what they were—emotions caused by ignorance. If you stooped to the same level, life would become one long succession of feuds. It was far better to overlook failings, although that didn't mean overlooking principle.

Our family acquired a reputation for apparent inconsistency—tough on some issues and easy on others. In reality, I think this approach was highly consistent. For generations we were taught to ignore the pettiness and ignorance that irritate on a personal level and work to better the situation. But if a principle was at issue, you stood like a rock to defend it. Unfortunately, few people these days think in those terms. They want to fight at the least provocation. A display of temper is appropriate and necessary as a response to injustice, but it must be carefully controlled and directed. You must separate conscience and convenience in motivation to understand another person's perspective.

Similarly, religion can be expressed several ways with the same intensity. Some people are compelled to give testimony as a matter of conviction. Others, like Dad, feel that one's beliefs are private and sacred. He taught us that you should respect the differences among people.

Dad used to say that the world is far too complex for anyone to claim that he completely understands it. By faith, he can know he is here for a purpose because he has been given freedom of choice and an intellect by his Creator. Although he might not understand the mysteries of God's creation, he must recognize that gifts also impose responsibilities. Dad believed he had a responsibility to use these choices wisely and to make his life meaningful in the short time allotted to him. Dad interpreted his responsibilities to include nurturing Deanna and me. Of his many roles, Dad considered family leadership to be one of his most meaningful contributions. It was, in a sense, a man's approach to immortality.

This is what I am trying to teach my son and daughters. I want them to understand how the world works. They need to learn the importance of citizenship and become aware of life at deeper levels. They should recognize the strength and unity that can emerge from being a family.

One way Dad led our family was by giving Deanna and me a perspective in life from history. He tried to show us how to recognize and organize historical events in order to understand how these influences affected us. He taught in simple and easy-to-understand stories, and I assumed that every father did the same thing. But since I have become a father, I now see how difficult it is to spend time communicating with my family and, most importantly, to convey the spiritual, cultural, and financial awareness that they must have in order to sustain themselves and have a positive effect on society through turbulent times. Society is only as strong as each individual. As each person becomes more balanced and develops a broadened perspective and more refined morality, our state and nation will improve. Improving civilization is a slow process, and it does not advance if evil dominates virtue.

As I surveyed the stars, picking out the basic constellations for the children, I was struck by the idea of a greater meaning to the word "power" than I had considered before. There is political and economic power. Religious and social institutions have power. Our society has given great power to its communications media. Basically, there is power in all aspects of living and thinking.

At the same time, however, I realized that I may have been under-estimating the impact and power of family. Families throughout the world differ in style and size. Our culture is based on the nuclear family of father, mother, and children. Other societies have extended families which can include entire villages. Despite these differences, the purpose and ultimate power of the family unit to *shape thought* and chart the course of civilization is astounding. It is also the basic unit in which the relationship with God can be most readily communicated and experienced. Sitting under the stars with my children, I felt I finally comprehended one of Dad's greatest lessons. Amid all the troubles and turbulence of life, the potential for our individual families to affect the course of human events is phenomenal. Perhaps through the character-building efforts of parents around the world, we *individually* possess one of the few *real* answers to solving the problems facing us. The greatest challenge is learning the truths of life and deciding what to teach.

My parents fostered a foundation of competency and belonging which Deanna and I have enjoyed in life. I learned to live with others and be a contributing citizen. My family's influence, combined with that of people I met through our community and church and others who played public roles in building Texas, illustrated a way to combine devotion and stewardship that I will never forget. These people helped form my basic philosophy that we can sustain our free society through our families. They showed me that education and a broadened perspective of life was crucial if we, as citizens, were to vote for and support statesmen to represent us in government. They instilled in me a sense of ethics and morality which must first be present in each *individual* citizen before we can recognize and demand these qualities in our leaders.

Passing on cultural values and an understanding of history is a delicate process. If culture is not taught to even one generation, we would probably return to Stone Age behavior. I remember seeing several movies based on real-life situations that depicted humans growing up alone or with animals in wild surroundings. Without the benefit of human interaction and education, these people behaved very much like animals. They did not have language or social skills and when they encountered our culture, they had difficulty adapting.

Families tend to influence society in Brenham as they do in any other city or town in the world. It seems that whenever any part of our inter-dependent society is positively or negatively affected, the family and all other institutions feel the impact. For example, Dad and Mother strongly believed that Deanna and I should be successful in school. They also provided a home which was comfortable and happy. We took these things for granted more often than not and failed to see how they fit into a larger scheme of life. Yet, soon after starting my own family, it became apparent to me how important a healthy family unit is to society.

Kitty and I feel that society will benefit if we encourage our children to achieve in school. Success in school will help them in business or whatever pursuits they choose to follow. As they become adult contributors to their community, their accomplishments in business or other endeavors can create jobs and income for themselves and other families. As was pointed out to me in scouting, good habits become a part of your being. Families with adequate cash flow tend to have less financial stress. They enjoy more opportunities to enrich their lives with travel, art, special training, and hobbies. Each member of the family has a better chance to develop a healthy self-image and positive self-esteem, which encourages them to help other people and improve society even more. Maintaining an adequate standard of living is essential to a family's well-being.

If we allow a business to make a fair profit, and the business works in harmony with the long-term interests of society, we have made a real contribution to ourselves and others. In an economic sense we have strengthened the family, because we have reduced some of the pressures that create friction. If we concentrate on long-term solutions to our economic woes, we will have a stronger economy in which the family is the first to benefit. Real prosperity increases leisure and gives us opportunity to spend more time with our families. A truly strong family is one in which every individual relationship has private time to develop.

When we were an agricultural society there was ample time to build family relationships. In fact, entertainment often centered around the family because there were few other things to do. Over the years, however, radio and television began to compete with family time. Video games followed as the pace of life accelerated. Now, many families devote more time chauffeuring kids to soccer practice, little league games, dancing lessons, and innumerable other activities than they spend having real fellowship with their children. Increased economic pressure often requires both parents to work outside the home, and little time is left for nurturing a solid marriage or children's needs. As a result, some areas of our country are experiencing very high divorce rates, and children are fleeing home for the streets of urban America. Parents often choose to leave their extended families of aunts, uncles, and grandparents and move to distant cities in search of more material benefits for their children or themselves. The solid foundation our families once provided for society is eroding.

The problems faced by modern families occur whenever any society is in a period of transition. When ancient Rome was declining, the family unit began to deteriorate and spirituality faded from true belief to empty ritual. As families weaken and religion stagnates, we can see from world history, as in the decline of Rome, that the fundamental underpinnings of morality collapse. I was taught that healthy and sound morality is the foundation on which individual responsibility is built. Individual responsibility is then the wellspring of a national will through which a country finds a common purpose and direction.

The changes and pressures within day-to-day life can be overpowering to families. We as parents are not always sure how to proceed in "training up a child in the way he should go." Mother and Dad were excellent role models for me, and I hope that I am providing the same sort of leadership and values for my children. Part of my parents' philosophy was derived from the Bible and their spiritual understanding of life. Another part came from the everyday experiences of seeing how the world operates and teaching Deanna and me the most effective values and techniques for having a fulfilling life. Some of the most important lessons I learned at home included discerning the abiding values in life that bring joy, the proper role of ambition, the wise use of leadership, personal excellence, and responsibility.

The way a family builds these values is through trust and respect, and these do not necessarily occur together. They have to be acquired over a long time. Individual acts are important but patterns are more significant.

One of the most difficult vacations I ever experienced brought home the importance of trust. Our family went to a dude ranch in Colorado. I wanted the kids to learn good horsemanship before I bought horses for our ranch. It was a well-intentioned effort designed to bring the children a little closer to their heritage and allow them to see some of the grand sights of nature. Tee, my only son, was eight and feared very little. He had ridden before, but had a hard time guiding a horse since his kicks went mainly to the saddle.

On the first morning Tee was given a big white horse named Snowball. We had been very impressed with the ranch's training program, which was world renowned, when we previewed it the previous summer. Meg was progressing with instruction, and little Buffy had buggy rides with a ranch counselor. At noon on the first day, however, Tee came back, threw his hat on the floor and said, "Dad, that horse hates me. I don't like him. I am not going back! He'll kill me!" I smiled and remembered how my dad had handled it when I had a "confidence crisis". I was sympathetic but said, "Tee, you have to go back. If you walk away, you'll never be strong. You have to face fears and conquer them." I explained to him how I had been afraid to speak publicly. I told him that winners have to summon courage, quit whining and try again. He agreed and went back, and I was pleased. That night, however, we had to repeat the whole scene again as Tee returned saying, "That horse hates me and I hate him. He's mean and no fun."

Reluctantly, he agreed to go back the next day after I promised that if it wasn't better he could quit after one last try. That morning I left early on an all-day ride with several friends. When we stopped to eat at noon, a friend of mine from Chicago joined me and commented, "You know, my son really likes Tee." That prompted an immediate smile of pride from me. "He says he is the bravest little boy he's ever met in his whole life." Impressed, I asked why. "Well, you know all the problems he had with that horse yesterday. In the morning he tried to roll over on Tee in the creek and chased him around a tree while nipping at him. But, by gosh, Tee came back in the afternoon. But then the horse ran away with him across a field until the guides finally caught up."

I was astounded because neither Tee nor the wranglers had mentioned any of this. I worried all the way back. Thankfully, when I returned Tee was fine. They had given him a new horse after the scares the previous day, and he was as happy as could be. I asked him why he had not told me all that had happened. He explained that he thought it was all part of riding a horse. He simply didn't have an adult's experience from which to judge.

This incident caused me to ponder about the credibility problems fathers have to face—such as the time we were having our house reroofed. The roofers started hammering on the roof at 6:30 A.M., and it scared Tee considerably. He woke me up, but I told him that there was nothing to fear. I suggested he watch television until I got up to fix breakfast. Believing me, he walked down the hall only to have the smoke alarm fall off the ceiling and hit him squarely on the head as a result of the vibration from the hammering.

Another time I had taken the kids fishing in Acapulco Bay. I told Tee and my daughter, Meg, that fish didn't bite, but to watch their fins. Just minutes after my assuring words, Meg caught a huge barracuda which immediately tore a piece of flesh out of the fishing guide's arm and then chased the kids across the deck while the guide was beating it to death.

Parents have to take special care to look at things from a child's perspective. At the same time parents have to realize it is easy to be in error on occasions as well. Trust is the only bridge that helps us get through those difficult times. And that trust makes possible and directs the formation of our children's values. Many children accept their parents' religion, views of morality and work ethic at a young age. If there is a vacuum in the home, then their impressions of society are formed by the perceptions they receive from outside forces.

I think our society tends to overemphasize monetary power, military might, business empires, and industrial prowess. Our values often have become distorted and unbalanced, and our children can easily absorb the wrong messages about personal worth. As a society, both men and women tend to view these symbols of power as the only praiseworthy achievements. People who succeed in these types of endeavors are overvalued in relation to others. Those who are not building businesses, industries or financial empires are often considered to have less worth to society. Children perceive this attitude through our culture, and it can have a great impact on them. Their fathers and mothers may not seem to live an exciting existence because they are not great risk-takers. Nonetheless, I remember well a quote my father often used : "It matters not what a man does; his profession doesn't give him merit. It is his character and how he lives his life that distinguish him."

I have known men in banking, real estate, oil and gas, and other professions who made great fortunes. Many times those fortunes were acquired more through luck than intelligence. People were in the right place at the right time and simply didn't understand the risks they were taking. Inflation made foolish men look like great financiers. Others were more conservative and cautious about their families' affairs. While they were willing to take some chances, they were not willing to risk their family's future, nor their children's education and security. Children are keen observers of their parents' behavior, and they quickly perceive whether their adult role models value material greed over the family's well-being.

I am not saying that ambition is unimportant. However, through our own actions we need to teach our children how to balance ambition with common sense and strive for a deeper perspective on life's values. I've tried to teach my children to do everything to the best of their ability and to realize that work done well and with commitment is honorable.

I think that when we as parents lead honorable lives, we foster a healthy sense of pride in our children. I was always proud of Mother and Dad, and I hope my children are able to look at our family with pride also. This is not the flashy facade that some try to project. Children can see through a charade, and they quickly lose respect for the adults in their lives who use it. I speak here about the pride that comes through living in harmony with other people and living according to a code of ethics in which we build society rather than detract from it.

The nurturing role of motherhood could benefit from a heightened sense of pride also. We often define achievement and honorable activity in terms of material power and undervalue the indispensable roles of mothering and homemaking. In society's myopic viewpoint, these activities seem to have little to do with building skyscrapers and vast industries. What we fail to acknowledge is that scores of women provide the foundation for their children to dream, achieve, and become the best that they can be.

Financial circumstances and the changing nature of modern times have affected many women's perspectives as they entered the work force. They saw that the way to gain recognition and fulfillment was to show what they were able to do in business, industry, and other traditionally male careers. It soon became apparent that gender had nothing to do with ability and mental prowess. The women's movement helped many develop self-esteem, and it elicited respect for their abilities. Of course, men also benefited. Increased family income provided greater opportunities, and we had the freedom to participate with our children and relate to them on a more sincere level. Unfortunately, I think that the movement away from the home has been too drastic. Some have suggested that when women left their full-time mothering roles they reinforced concepts which detracted from the value of home life and development of future generations.

I think I see, however, a change in the pendulum's direction. As both parents were removed from home, we began to see how difficult it was to balance each family member's spiritual and mental growth within a solid family environment while achieving success in other fields. I don't think anyone wants to return to the time when women had limited opportunities to develop their gifts. What we must find is a new balance that brings back the closeness and satisfaction of a past period. To do that we need to understand some of the basics for the changes and recognize that today's life styles will change family patterns and relationships. In many ways, that offers opportunity because the individuals are broadened and strengthened by taking more responsibility. Thus, it is not the "sameness" of family life that we want to retain, but rather "oneness" or "closeness" that provides feelings of warmth and security. With effort, that can be achieved, and it can help guide us along many paths more intelligently.

We are all familiar with the movement toward social equality for all people that has characterized this transition since the 1950s. Another important but perhaps unrecognized influence on the family is the role of international economics. The family's quality of life, lifestyle, and the amount of discretionary income available to educate children and broaden their horizons with activities and travel are tied to the household income.

After World War II, many Americans enjoyed a very high standard of living relative to the rest of the world. But other nations have slowly rebuilt and caught up with the United States, as we will examine in later chapters. Every family wants its children to have the same or a better education and lifestyle than the parents had. If they cannot achieve that goal, parents may feel they have failed their children. For that reason, we have struggled in recent years to maintain our standard of living, while we were consuming at greater levels than we as a nation were producing. In addition to economic competition at the international level was the competition produced by the "baby boom" generation with more people competing for fewer good jobs.

To maintain the family's standard of living, a breadwinner might take a second job or look for outside investments; but the nation as a whole has responded in three ways. First, Americans reduced family size to maintain the standard of living. Then mothers went to work to maintain a desired income level. And finally, we have resorted to the family going into debt to maintain its lifestyle. But debt has its limits, and the world of the future will be more competitive than the past. Even though we will become more productive as the baby boom generation reaches maturity, we face many competitive challenges. We have to make choices and value judgments. We can try to work much harder for more income, but that will continue to pull us further from the family. We can be satisfied with a simple family life and change our definition of success. Money buys a lot, but once you have achieved a certain level of affluence, the value of money is not that great. Some people may want to earn great fortunes to leave to their children—a noble goal, but one that can be a problem in itself if it removes the incentive for their children to be active in the world. Too often, if a person is primarily money-oriented and tells his family how hard it is to acquire wealth, the children spend their lives trying to conserve it without making any mistakes. They fear to venture out and often fail to gain the confidence they need. I aspire to leave my children enough funds to assure the best education possible and to guarantee their welfare with an opportunity to grow through their own abilities. But I want them to have that strong base of confidence that a family provides, so they will be able to venture on their own. This may become even more important to our children because they cannot automatically expect an ever-rising standard of living as we have had. Looking at the more mature economies of Europe in which new job creation is limited, one sees that the young face long and difficult job paths with the possibility of downward adjustments in the average standard of living. In America we will be helped by demographics that for the first time see labor shortage rather than surplus. If we choose wise economic policies, we may arrest what could be a very negative trend; but whether our standard of living increases or decreases, a renewed concentration on the family is necessary.

So for the sake of our society's long-term health and happiness, I believe that we need to re-evaluate the family's importance and find ways to adjust our lives to bring the home into center focus. A pendulum swings to its limits before settling within the center. I hope we will see our values shift from absorption in work by both parents to greater value placed on the home as a source of satisfaction and expression. As more time is spent on family and growth, hopefully less responsibility will be given to schools and day care centers for providing the mental, emotional, and spiritual stimulation for our children. I feel that both parents will then regain their rightful leadership in shaping their children's destiny as the new generation reaches maturity. This responsibility has to be assumed knowledgeably. Children often imitate their parents, but if we do not take time to explain why we do things in certain ways, they have no real basis of understanding. Their mental processes can then be filled by others who may have different values.

My mother and father exhibited the kind of leadership in our family that made for quality time. They saw the importance of raising us in an emotionally secure home. One of the ways they brought us together was through the Boy Scout and Girl Scout programs. My parents saw the scouting work as an opportunity to challenge and mentally prepare us for life. Scouting helped us develop constructive habits and such character traits as personal responsibility, dedication, and leadership. It was like learning how to skate, swim, or ride a bike. We don't usually remember when we learned those skills. They are like habits which are gradually acquired over time through repetition. In the same way, the values of hard work and dedication to accomplishing an end are at the very core of the scouting movement, and that training can set the course of a person's entire life. I applied myself in earnest as a scout and as a result earned my Eagle and Three Palms ranks. I thought Mother was happy because I had gotten the awards, but I later realized that the awards themselves were relatively insignificant to her. It was my effort and dedication in accomplishing a task that really mattered.

Mother and Dad approached our education with the same standards as they held for us in scouting. Although they put a great deal of emphasis on making good grades, the most important thing was that we achieved to the fullest of our abilities. Their leadership of our school careers is something which I have tried to emulate with my children. As I see it, the amount of ambition, drive and desire which children develop is determined in their families. If we provide this generation's children with the proper intellectual and moral preparation to deal intelligently with the new challenges of technology, space exploration, and human relations, then we will be doing a good job of conveying the principles of personal responsibility, self government and morality which will help them later on in life. Success in one field is success in another. Just as the cream rises to the top and separates from the milk, some people succeed at whatever they do. Often the people who were leaders in high school or college tend to assume leadership positions in society. Frequently this is not directly related to their inherent abilities, but to the degree that they actually use them.

If you have been in scouting, you know that personal responsibility is an important part of the program. However, I believe that the rewards of personal responsibility must be reinforced in the home. To me this means doing one's best, helping others, contributing to society, and fulfilling every obligation assumed. This is the key to living in harmony with other people. It is a path toward improving society and needs to be exercised by everyone if our entire culture is to be enriched. If we teach this in our families, we will directly influence industry, business, and government. Personal responsibility makes life interesting. It gives color and meaning to our everyday activities and motivates us to take responsibility for our own life, society, and world. As a result, we raise important questions, enter into debates, seek to influence others for the betterment of society, and strive to make a richer and more meaningful life for ourselves and others as well.

A democracy is based on individual responsibility, while the goal of a dictatorship is to make every citizen follow directions and orders without thinking. However, even within our free society, the exercise of personal responsibility is sometimes discouraged when our questions or suggestions disturb the status quo. Schools, churches, industry, business and government can either suppress or actively encourage and reward personal initiative and concern by their attitude toward constructive criticism. Ideas are often strenuously opposed by intimidation and negativism; open questioning and lively debate give them life and vitality. Individual responsibility forms the basis of the morality, which in turn sustains our social order. If we exercise personal responsibility in every judgement and concern, then we will react with it in our jury service, in our expectations of business, and in our political process.

Another trait that I have tried to help my children develop is a desire for personal excellence. If democracy is to survive, our society as a whole needs to recognize the importance of personal excellence, merit, and superior performance. Mediocrity has seldom achieved anything great. As William James said in 1906, "The true wealth of a nation consists more than anything else in the number of superior men that it harbors."

James Gardner, champion of excellence in the free society, said:

> "Those who are most deeply devoted to a democratic society must be precisely the ones who insist upon excellence, who insist that free men are capable of the highest standard of performance, who insist that a free society can be a great society in the richest sense of that phrase. The ideas for which this nation stands will not survive if the highest goal free men can set themselves is an amiable mediocrity."

Mother and Dad taught the same basic concept through their own lives and family leadership. They emphasized that once the pursuit of excellence becomes part of our character, we experience a keener sense of joy in our homes, workplaces, and civic activities. Most people will not be great political or business leaders, but if they are proficient and strive for excellence in their own fields, they contribute significantly to a general uplifting of society. I have noticed that people who pursue excellence have common characteristics. They sincerely try to practice integrity, honesty, and genuineness in their relationships with others. They go beyond limits set by society and measure their work by their own internal yardstick. They are patient and thorough. Striving for excellence expands their imagination and ability to visualize future possibilities. They recognize that the easiest way is not necessarily the best way. They experiment with new approaches to thinking and behavior and develop different ways of looking at old problems. These people tend to be constructive problem solvers, far more interested in the business approach of making money *with* someone rather than making money *off* someone. They realize that working together is usually more productive than tearing each other down. They understand the workings of cause and effect and seek solutions from a long-term point of view.

I particularly remember when my first grade teacher told Mother that I would probably be a "B" student. At this early age, I heard society's message that we should be content with less than excellent performance. Many of us receive a similar message from our teachers, religious leaders, and parents. Fortunately, Mother and Dad corrected that error quickly and gave me a glimpse of what pursuing excellence was all about. That inspired me to move forward and reach for ever higher goals. The best students were not always the smartest, but often they were the

most dedicated. It is the same in academics as it is in athletics. Those
with the greatest desire make the most use of their abilities and rise
above others with even more natural talent.

The United States began with a vision of excellence, of pursuing a
better and more ideal life. Since World War II, however, it seems to me
that we have begun to accept mediocrity. It could be that people were
lulled into mediocrity by the mass-production mentality of our technological society. Craftsmanship has waned, and there is little distinction in
our lives. Affluence in itself can reduce the drive for greater success because need wanes. I am concerned that our school systems may contribute to this lowering standard of excellence. Students often must endure
boredom in the classroom, not because the teacher isn't able to teach, but
simply because he or she is hamstrung by a wide range of abilities in the
class. Individual instruction often is not available, and a certain level of
mediocrity is accepted because that is the most cost-effective way to run
a school. But new avenues are opening to us through technology if we are
smart enough to grasp them. For example, Billy Reagan, former superin-
tendent of the Houston Independent School District, championed one of
education's most ambitious computer software experiments. Excellent
phonics software is used to teach language skills. Numerous children are
able to work on the same concepts at different levels. I believe this one
example illustrates incredible options for overcoming mediocrity by
providing more individualized instruction for each student. This becomes
essential when we realize that many nations, particularly Japan, emphasize education far more than we do. Japanese schools have longer terms
and higher admission standards. Great emphasis is placed on success. We
do our children no favors by being easy on them, knowing they face better
prepared competition that will affect their standard of living for the future.

However, in order for any school program to be successful, parents
need to be actively involved in their children's education, and society as a
whole needs to foot the bill. People often complain about low educational
standards and favor movements for improving education. Passage of the
Texas educational reform bill in 1985 indicated our concern. Everyone is
for excellence, but few want to pay for it. There is always a high price for
excellence. By our action and inaction, we have shown that respect for
education still is not given enough priority for us to recognize its value
and willingly pay that price. If we do not agree to strengthen our schools,
we will eventually suffer the consequences through a weakened economy.
Other nations, more dedicated to excellence, will rise, and our freedoms
will decrease in like measure. Life is made up of free will and choices. We
are in the process of making our choices and forging the chains of our

future. In a democracy, decay is less a result of brute force than the out-come of subtle choices to be less than we are capable of being.

As parents we must see that the education our children receive is meaningful not only in the commitment to learning, but also with regard to the content. Everyone supports education, but education is a "buzz word" for a grand policy. Too often we look only at the policy and not the strategies of how to administer the funds and programs. Money is often wasted by duplication, lack of coordination, and a lack of distinct planning. In these difficult times, we cannot cut back on our commitment to the best possible education. But we may well need to reassess how the ad-ministrators prioritize goals and spend money. Schools are second only to the family in influencing and preparing our children and our society. Un-less we are willing to be directly involved, they will become insular for lack of broad outside influences. Schools naturally emphasize teaching when the real issue is learning. And most critical of all, students must learn skills which fit into the economy of the future so they can build and support their families. Parents have to get involved, not just in parent/teacher organization activities, but through participation in the broader governmental and political policies where the real direction is set through funding. However, they must do so knowledgeably. If they only do so emotionally, they will cause more problems than benefits. In the future, there will be larger groups of people without children in public school, and they will tend to oppose heavier spending unless they see overall value for the expenditures. So the perception of education must be changed from a "teaching babysitter" function to what it truly is—the future of our economy which builds the cultural values of our society and the unify-ing force that propels and forms a national will and destiny.

Another concept that I am trying to instill in our children is the im-portance of balanced perspective and activity in all areas of their lives. During family discussion times, we sometimes talk about things they are learning in their classes in order to help them develop interest and focus on important points. Scientific discovery is multiplying at an ever faster rate. For example, the simple atom which I learned about years ago has been found to be a much more complicated particle. The field of chemis-try once was seen as an ingenious way to create fertilizers and medi-cines. While technology is zooming ahead, I am concerned that our spiri-tual and moral growth may be lagging behind. During our conversations, I try to give our children another perspective from which to judge the use of new technology. I feel very strongly that the family unit needs to pro-vide an arena to discuss these issues and at the same time give children a spiritual perspective. That point of view is crucial for balancing their awareness that all new technology must be seen in the light of moral and spiritual principles. If the family does not do its job in giving children a solid ethical foundation, we may sadly discover that our discoveries will become new weapons in the hands of the fearful and greedy.

Technology is good if it increases leisure time, and we spend our extra hours in life-long education, good works, and inner growth. A balanced citizen who enjoys a broadened perspective requires leisure to learn and reflect. However, if leisure time is wasted, then technology will continue to outpace us, and what we don't control would eventually dominate us. If we allow the distance between technology and personal character to widen, we may be unprepared to make humane decisions on the use of that technology. When personal character development is stunted, technology will continue to be used for war, destruction and enslavement. Technology should not be perceived as an enemy. It can be used far more beneficially to enhance the quality of life and learning. The characteristics of integrity, good will and morality are absolutely essential to ensure that technology is used properly. Understanding the wisdom of morality is as important as possessing the knowledge of technology.

Encouraging morality and spiritual faith in one's family is crucial because a child's perspective on all aspects of life, including his self-image and role as a responsible citizen in a democratic country, is influenced by such a foundation. Like Dad, I believe the family fills the house, but God makes the home. Likewise, people populate a nation, but it is God's love which inspires and leads them in morality, brotherly love, and righteousness.

Many of our family's ancestors came to Texas from Europe more for religious than economic reasons. I tell my children that while they received a legacy from these people, they also have a spiritual legacy which they can claim through their own free choice. That new legacy comes from God. If a child is adopted, he becomes heir to a new legacy from another family. Likewise, we have an opportunity to be adopted into a spiritual family, and thus receive God's legacy. It is one of my desires that we, as a nation of individuals and families, will turn to God, seek His wisdom and guidance, and live, as a nation, within His will—not as sects and denominations riddled with conflicts, but rather as men and women who exhibit His love in their lives. Then we will be blessed individually and as a nation.

It seems as though some people today have created a grey area between right and wrong which never existed in simpler times. While I encourage my children to think critically and independently, I still present them with a very clear concept of right and wrong. I tell them that it is necessary to stand firm when they are right rather than to give in to pressure, and I teach them to acknowledge when they are wrong and to be willing to change their ways.

For example, many people would argue that we must restrict the use of all guns and that the building of a mighty military arsenal is improper. Unfortunately, as Machiavelli noted in *The Prince,* it is often necessary for those who would do good to understand how evil is done. If we are not strong, we will not be respected. The secret is to remain strong in a self-defensive posture, but to be extremely affirmative and confident in selling our ideas and values. Dad used to say that a handshake and a smile were the best things with which to make any new man a friend. But he also noted that "a pistol on the hip never did any harm." I believe the argument should not just focus on whether to disarm, but instead on how we can convey our ideas more forcefully than the opposition in order to win them over to our way of thinking.

I hope that as I talk to my children about issues which will confront them as adults, I will be successful in teaching them the importance of balance in everything they do. Socrates said that when people lose touch with the human values of integrity and moderation, their democracies will drift into a well-meaning and unintentional chaos where balanced and moderated freedoms yield to increasing demands for self-gratification. Then, at some point, citizens will eagerly allow a tyrant to rule them as a way to force society into an artificial order to control citizens who can't control themselves.

This balance between freedom and license rests on a very delicate line. The goal is to allow as much personal freedom as possible in order to free the human mind, body and spirit to achieve its greatest potential, while at the same time not allowing people to impose on the lives and rights of other citizens. If you are a parent, you probably have ample opportunity to teach this particular lesson. One of the hardest things to teach a child seems to be that his freedom stops where the other person's nose begins. However, children emulate their parents. Families who treat their children with respect and consideration create adults who reciprocate that philosophy with others in their environment and demand high values from government and business. This type of respect creates a society with its own internalized norms of personal freedom and restraint. Its citizens are able to control themselves and have little desire to give up control of their lives to others. Personal responsibility is required on the part of each individual citizen in order to maintain this balance. If we think that our government agencies and courts will do this for us or that our institutions will do it alone, then we are trying to live as powerless children in the care of bureaucrats, dependent upon these institutions for our lives. Always remember that those bureaucrats and judges are just like us.

Another important characteristic of a healthy and balanced society, which the family has an ideal opportunity to teach, is appreciation and concern for the minority opinion. Whether it involves a decision on what television program to watch or whether the family will relocate to a new city, someone will often hold a viewpoint not shared by others. Whether this happens in a family or a society as a whole, the majority needs to be sensitive to the minority viewpoint. Balance brings stability.

When individualism deteriorates into looking out for "Number One" we begin to think that as long as we get what pleases and benefits us, the highest good has been achieved and the losers can fend for themselves. It is the difference between trying to achieve the good for all concerned versus the good for the greatest number. The "greatest number" implies that there will be a minority of people who do not receive what they consider to be their greatest good or fair share. Hopefully, we can find other ways to achieve what they need. If all other avenues are closed to them, they may live quietly for a while, yet history shows that the minority never disappears. They just get shoved aside to breed resentment and hurt, later to reappear with intensified strength of conviction and ready to do battle to the degree necessary. When this involves a family, a child who feels as though he or she is always in the minority might resort to unacceptable actions.

Often the majority's short-sighted perspective never considers this inevitable cycle. Too often when the loser's voice is finally heard in a political, economic, or social upset, the tables are turned and the winner is toppled. The loser then recreates the same pitiful conditions which become the breeding ground for more chaos. It is to a degree the rubber band theory—as far to one extreme as a rubber band proceeds, it normally proceeds back with equal strength to the other. In politics, when an elected official becomes a "poor winner" and does not unite constituencies, but instead tries to punish his opposition, the distrust and ill will that are created immediately breed resentment that normally leads to his defeat in a following election.

The same principle is as true for business as it is in the family or politics. A business will never be successful for an extended period of time when it mistreats workers or customers. Inappropriate practices that are not remedied by higher level management will normally be corrected by outside regulators and the courts. Regulations do not simply appear; they come in recognition of a potential need and a lack of balance within a process. Similarly, as labor more fully recognizes that it is only entitled to the direct fruits of its labor based on the profitability of its products, it will more actively join, and in some cases force management, in changing competitive approaches. Strong and stable economic growth can occur without international competition destroying the jobs and businesses of all concerned. Business can pay no more than it is able to make, and the realities of life have to be addressed.

This fact is recognized far more today than it was ten years ago. There is more cooperation and balance within society because it has been forced upon us by international competition, but new areas of imbalance always emerge. There is also a natural law that says that for every action there is a reaction. By observing the events of life, we can see the truth of that principle. Its recognition is one of the most important things that we can teach our children. If we look at the potential consequences of our actions, we might not make the mistakes that we have in the past.

In summary, the balance which is required within society grows from morality and the teachings and perspectives of the family unit which shaped each of us as individuals. If we were treated fairly and every family member lived by the golden rule, we will treat others with the same respect. The balance within society that often must be found from the swinging of the pendulum in different directions could have far less devastating effects if that sense of fairness kept it from moving so widely. The family is the key for instilling the characteristics that we have discussed. All of them are important, and the concepts could be considered from thousands of directions. The critical point is that there are relationships which are formed between all of the members within a family and if values are not taught, if pride and trust do not exist, then there is little hope that society as a whole will be any stronger.

Character is destiny for individuals as well as nations. If character is not taught, it will not be acquired. It is very important, then, to recognize the significance of a strong family unit within our society and the part it plays within our future. If we talk in terms of molding our society from the roots, each of us needs to recognize that we need to reshape our lives in order to give the family greater precedence. Dad felt that God and family were critically important to the nation. They are the first priorities of life. Following those are government, politics, special interests, and all of the other lesser items that clamor for our attention while we are here on earth. I believe that if we choose, we can adopt that system of priority in our lives. We have control of our lives. If we spend our time simply in the pursuit of money, that becomes our god. If we spend it fulfilling ambition, we have surrendered to personal pride. If we want to build and enjoy life to the fullest, we need satisfaction, and perhaps one of the few ways that we know satisfaction is through the inner feeling of having made correct choices according to our own priorities.

Some of us may occasionally wish that we could return to those times of our youth when things were not so complex; when questions and answers seemed much simpler, and most important of all, when we felt we had an inner happiness and closeness. We seek this far more as we begin to recognize our own mortality, a realization that is certainly taking place within the generation of the post-World War II baby boomers. We want the best of life for our children and with our children. We see them growing up much too fast, and we want to make sure that we don't lose precious years that cannot be reclaimed in building relationships. The one important thing about the family is that we have the power to make it one of life's top priorities. Through our families we wield tremendous impact on life, and we thereby have the power to make significant changes in society. But first we need the *will* to do it and a recognition of the characteristics which go into building a family.

It is said that a busy man is the one you choose to get a job done, because somehow he will make the time. The same is true in creating the proper types of relationships within our families and taking the time to teach new generations. Time has a tyranny all its own if it is not checked. Almost everyone remembers the family vacations of his childhood. In part it was the excitement of new places, but beyond that it was a time of true family togetherness. Pressures were removed from normal existence, and the family was truly together. We take family vacations at every opportunity. Every individual relationship in a family must have its own time to fully develop; there is no greater priority than creating the proper opportunity for that to occur.

The location of a vacation is not as important as spending quality time with each other. This is when real teaching can take place rather than in the rush of daily life. It is the same the world over because family life and relationships are a common phenomenon to all people.

Each of us needs to ask when the last time was that we sat with a child and looked at the stars and explained to them that there are many secrets in the universe, or went into a field and looked at the flowers, the trees, and the grasses and contemplated the great complexities that create the world as we know it. It was not happenstance; it did not just occur. The sciences are discovering far more things in common with the Bible than we ever thought possible.

I have always been amazed that concrete in its powdered state seems to have far less strength than sand. Water can be added to both, but in one case there is a bonding and in the other only drainage. Values are like the powdered concrete which, when combined with proper ingredients, becomes as strong as rock.

The strength and potential of those values may not be obvious in the beginning, but the results inevitably show. If we are to be a society of concrete will, which can achieve excellence and bring out the best in all of our people, then we must start at the beginning of life in the smallest unit of society—the family. What may seem of small value to some will inevitably become the most important.

The America we knew is dying, but a second America is rising from the body of the first. This second nation— America II—can best be seen in the South and West. . . . The second America is a state of mind: a powerful yearning for opportunity, for old values and new technologies, for refuge and escape.

—RICHARD LOUV, *AMERICA II*

III.

TEXAS IN TRANSITION

Some of the best times I remember while growing up in Brenham were the hunting trips which Dad and I took with other men from our town. It was on those trips that I learned much about life and how the world works. As dusk settled in we would build a campfire, cook dinner, and start a game of poker. I liked to listen to Dad and the other men talk about the old days when they served together in World War II or how their families survived the Great Depression. Thinking back on those camps always fills me with a sense of pride about Texas—where we have been and where we will be in the future. Many people think rural Texas is a backwoods area lacking the sophistication of the east or the glamour of the west coast. But rural Texas has values and a type of homespun logic which gives a more practical education than some might imagine. It provides an education of common sense rather than white papers, wordy dissertations, or blue ribbon committees. The men who sat around Dad's campfires had just fought World War II. They had sacrificed a great deal and appreciated the importance of personal character, national will, and the strength of ideas and values. They had been through the crucible of pressure, and they knew how it had fortified them and the nation as a whole. Dad was always concerned that those lessons would be lost on my generation because we had not experienced an economic depression or a major war. He saw trends in government and society which he felt were breaking down the work ethic, family values, and the way of life in Texas which had helped forge a special character of surviving despite the odds.

This was the legacy of Texas which Dad had passed to me. Now it was my responsibility to make my own way in life. Kitty and I had decided to return to Brenham after serving in the Navy. Through those years of our personal change and growth, Texas was undergoing a transition too. Many of the men who wrote to the family after Dad's passing were important agents of this change in Texas. People like Governor Allan Shivers and Governor John Connally taught me about the interrelationships of politics and economics and how these elements affect our daily lives. John Ben Shepherd taught me the meaning of devotion, and he inspired many to work for the continued betterment of Texas. He also showed that far more could be accomplished working as a team with others than individually.

As a result of keen insights into the connections between economics and politics, these people were able to influence ideas and set trends which furthered our Texas traditions. At times, however, they broke tradition when it seemed to be in our best interests. Governor Allan Shivers did this when he decided to break ranks with the Democratic Party in the 1950s and support the Republican candidate for president, Dwight Eisenhower.

The major observation of these men and others was this: *It is crucial to know where we are going.* Knowing what happened yesterday is vital, and we need to understand today's economics and political situation. But even more importantly, we need to know where we are heading as individuals, as a state, and as a nation. We not only need to know where trends project us, but what we can do to affect them in positive ways. This understanding helps build the vital personal and national will to sacrifice for positive change. These leaders passed a worthy legacy to all of us. Yet our current challenges are formidable, and change is happening faster than we can, at times, accommodate comfortably.

It is now incumbent upon all of us to shape and control the future of our dreams. Texas is a state of tradition, a tradition which encourages thought and new ideas. And most important to our collective well-being, it is a state which embraces new people and opportunity. Texans are no less American than other groups, they just have a special set of strong values. These values are common to many and worthy of preservation. The blending of traditional values with entrepreneurial spirit and a newly

educated generation makes Texas a unique state even as it suffers economically from the oil price crash of the 1980s. There is a synergism of
events that makes this a worthwhile study both for dedicated Texans who
want the best future possible and for non-Texans who can identify with
the evolutionary beginning of a third coast of thought.

In Texas we must commit ourselves to the task of creating a new
legacy for our children's children. Each one of us plays a part in that responsibility, and I hope that these thoughts will encourage continued dia-
logue. Ultimately, we can only do and achieve what we sincerely desire as
a people. Offered in that spirit, my thoughts are suggested avenues for
reaching what we as Texans have as a common goal. In a democracy,
every person's thoughts and needs deserve a voice, but unless we mani-
fest them, they will die on the vine, and we will all lose the freedom our
forefathers nurtured and cherished. As time moves forward, Texas again
will emerge as a major economic and political force in our nation. It is a
cohesive state because Texans firmly grasp ideas even though they may
not recognize them as such on occasion. This combination of commitment
to ideas and our sense of unity can make Texas pivotal in the course of
national and international events. What is critically important to our finding the right path for the state's future is that our children learn to recognize the importance of that path and keep on it even as the world
changes. Like the North Star, a common point of reference is invaluable.

Dad used to say that historical events often don't shape our future
as much as the interrelationships of power which gradually change our
perceptions. We may start with one set of relationships, but the world is
dynamic, not static. It can move in both positive and negative directions.
If we understand economics, politics, media, and family—we can bring
more depth, perspective, and integrity into our world through effective
communication. As a banker, I've watched the quiet shift in the public's
thinking and how it has affected the economy. Our opinions have impact on politicians who make changes in government by increasing regulation or taxation. Media sources communicate how government is affecting our personal lives, and we respond positively or negatively to that
information.

I refuse to accept the opinion of the cynics who say it is naive to
believe we can bring more maturity, honor, and principle to politics. I've
seen how people can influence each sector of our economy without fully
realizing their impact on the other parts of society. We can bring the positive values of limited government and respect for opportunity back into
the forefront of political thinking and encourage statesmen to succeed in

politics. However, a statesman's success, and our consequent benefit, can be achieved only if we grasp the relationship between key ideas affecting our society.

In many ways, the Texas that existed in Brenham 30 years ago is gone. If you've lived in Texas for awhile, you've seen the change. Several years ago, revenue from oil was flowing into our state treasury. We were blessed with having to decide what to do with all of it. But that has changed. Texas is moving into the international market, and our ways of looking at life will be changed as a result. We will no longer be able to rest easily on oil and gas revenue. Our products and services will have to compete with Germany, Japan, Taiwan, and other nations. And some of our time-honored values will be questioned by people who are new arrivals.

Fortunately in the face of change, we are still holding onto most of the proven traditions, although sometimes it feels like our grip might be slipping. We still appreciate the family and its central role in keeping Texas strong and healthy. We are patriotic. Our religious beliefs and practices are still important parts of our daily lives.

But change is like water—it can wash away mountains and cut valleys where there were none. Texas has been fortunate to have a number of men and women who have seen change coming, and they have had the courage to move our state forward. These changes and new trends occur throughout society. I believe the best way to structurally analyze them is by looking at politics, economics, and communication. By understanding and watching how these elements affect each other, we can often observe specific trends in each of them.

Texas has been in an economic tailspin through most of the 1980s, and concerns about the economy dominate discussion and usually cloud future vision. However, by understanding the arenas of power, we can get a more accurate handle on what choices we really have for the future as well as the different kind of future we now face. We can then better discern between our own perceptions and reality. This will allow us to plan for the future more effectively. Today, the likelihood is higher prices in the future coupled with significant short-term deficits. We are faced with choices about whether to increase taxes, cut services, or find other ways to expand our revenues—options that might differ if we take a short versus long-term perspective of what is best.

In 1986, I served as a member of the Economic Advisory Committee to Texas House Speaker Gib Lewis. This committee brought together nearly all of the major Texas think tanks and research institutes with assistance from state agencies and universities. The committee's purpose was to discover facts and gain a perspective from which solutions could be formed. Since almost all tax legislation must originate in the House, the Speaker's concern about the economic plight of Texas is vital.

Drs. Bernard Weinstein and Harold Gross of the SMU Center for Enterprising prepared a report entitled, *The Texas Economy in Transition: Causes, Implication, and Policy Responses,* for the Speaker's Economic Advisory Committee. This report presented startling statistics on the changes confronting our state.

Drs. Weinstein and Gross spoke of four structural changes which will have profound impact on Texas. These changes are in energy, agriculture, high-technology, and demography. In regard to demographic changes, Weinstein and Gross said:

> "With declining birthrates throughout the nation, the single most important factor in population redistribution has become interregional migration, in particular net migration or the difference between the number of people moving into and out of a state. For example, during the 1970s and early 1980s, population growth in Texas averaged 3 percent annually, more than triple the nation's growth rate. But nearly 40 percent of Texas' population growth during this period was the result of net in-migration. Between 1980 and 1982 alone 600,000 more people moved into the state than out.
>
> At present, however, net migration is close to zero, a consequence of Texas' economic downturn combined with the aging of the U.S. population. For the next decade, population growth in Texas will come primarily from natural increase."

Now that the tide of immigration has slowed, newcomers to Texas will decide whether to stay or leave our state. Some of them will stay because they like the values, the weather, and the Texan viewpoint. Others who came for the short-term economic opportunity have gone or will do so when they can. But the new Texans who stay will add to and strengthen that unique character, because that is what appeals to them.

A lot of these people are like the waves of immigrants who came to Texas from nations around the world and other parts of the United States in the 1800s. We all have come in pursuit of the American Dream—in Texas. Whether your family has lived in Texas for generations or you have just moved here from another state or country, we are all a part of that dream. It is a vision of being everything that each one of us can be. It is expansion of our personal boundaries. For some people that means material success. Others think it means to expand their minds and intellects, and for a large number of people, it means to expand spiritually. Some came for job opportunity or simply because they liked the weather. But most came to Texas because something inside them, a vague yearning for a sense of freedom, beckoned them here; being Texan is not so much a matter of birthplace as attitude. The state's tradition of limited government fosters an attitude of individual opportunity to succeed or fail.

In this day of economic difficulty that opportunity is not so clear in the short-term. But the Texas character will still shape our long-term government policies. Ever since the frontier days, each new wave of immigration has taken its toll on the land and lifestyles of earlier inhabitants. There has been a constant transition from established lifestyles and thinking to new ways of earning a living—learning to cooperate with others and communicating new ideas.

Regardless of whether we are new or long-time Texans, we are all faced with an economy in transition. This change really started in the early 1970s. The first boost in oil prices had taken place, and we experienced increased wealth and job opportunities. Texas not only had rich mineral resources, we also had an extremely large petrochemical industry, built during World War II so that the refineries would be close to the oil fields reducing the cost and time of transportation. Texas was beginning to look out at the world, and we were venturing into internationalism and moving away from being a provincial agricultural state of cattle and cotton. Our oil was creating wealth not only in the energy industry but in all industries affected by it—real estate to banking to other services. It was an example of what President Reagan later called the "trickle-down theory"—which, in one sense, holds that all businesses tend to rise when one area of an economy improves.

Recent events show they can fail as well, as the "Texas in Transition" report explains:

> "What is playing out in the 1980s is a reversal of forces that benefitted the state during the 1970s. Texas was a regional beneficiary of the high inflation rates that characterized the 1970s. As is always the case during the inflationary periods, commodity prices rose faster than those of fabricated products; so Texas received more for the energy and agriculture products it sold relative to the prices it paid for finished goods produced in other regions. The result was a substantial transfer of real income from other sections of the U.S. to Texas. The 1980s, by contrast, has been a deflationary period with commodity prices dropping to a much greater extent than prices for finished goods. The income and wealth shift is now in the opposite direction with the traditional industrial heartland of the Northeast and Midwest benefitting from lower commodity prices and higher real income."

Drs. Weinstein and Gross predict that energy-related employment will continue to decrease in Texas. They tell us that there is overcapacity in our refineries and petrochemical plants. That situation, combined with less demand for refined petrochemical products and foreign competition, will continue to shrink refining industry jobs by 50,000 workers through the year 2000. Much of the employment loss will be in Texas. In 1981, most energy economists were predicting that the price of oil would go as high as $85 per barrel by 1985. Increases in the price of oil encouraged rampant worldwide exploration and production. The world soon became awash in a sea of oil as producers sought to capture as much petroleum earnings as possible. The result was the tumbling of oil prices and a devastating ripple effect on our economy. Even as OPEC agrees to stabilize production and, therefore, oil prices, the outlook for a significant short-term rise in oil prices is remote. In the long-term, conservation, energy alternatives, and the lessons of the last "energy" boom will temper surges.

Texas has always had an almost obsessive urge to export our ideas about sound economics to the rest of the world. But right now the world is watching to see if we can pull ourselves through the decline in the energy industry without raising taxes drastically. *The style and logic of the approach we take is as important to that cause as what bills are passed.* Waste must be cut, but a clear, precise vision for the future has to be instilled. A sense of dedication to a long-range committed course of action Just emerge to give people confidence. The report to the Speaker of the House goes on to say:

> "Just as the oil industry fueled Texas' industrialization during the 1970s and early 1980s, it also fueled state spending programs and allowed legislators and taxpayers the luxury of not having to pass tax increases or grapple with such controversial issues as a state, corporate, or personal income tax. Conversely, the state's recent "deindustrialization" brought on by declining oil prices and the restructuring in refining and petrochemicals, coupled with the structural inflexibility Lf a tax system wedded to energy-based prosperity, has brought heretofore unimagined fiscal problems."

Texans have always had the strength to tighten their belts when the going got tough and stick to doing things the right way—such as not spending more than we bring in and keeping state government lean. But we have had some pretty fat years, and government expanded greatly during that period. We now have had several legislative sessions of "belt-tightening." The big question is whether we're going to stick to our traditions of sound economics or give in to the "politics of desperation" that often occur when there is no consensus but people know that something must be done. Concepts of "no taxes" or "full services" budgets are offered. But the real issue is broader than those ideas. Government is not an individual or business which "tightens its belt" when everyone else does. It often tends to be countercyclical. When business is bad, government is inundated with requests for unemployment relief, welfare, health benefits or other services because demands are greater, and the private sector is least able to assist. Cutting long-term projects like education becomes a temptation.

However, times of crisis bring focus on waste and misdirection of funds in all areas, so "belt-tightening" is a two-edged sword. We can easily cut muscle rather than fat, but we can also use the argument of compassion for momentary needs, and thereby burden ourselves and the system to make it unproductive. *The fine decision line comes from having a style or approach to government that envisions a broader goal of what relationship we expect government to have with the people.* While that sounds like a simple concept, it is seldom appreciated. Unless we have a goal, how can we judge the benefit of any action?

The decision to trim the fat and tighten our belts will be made by the people through our representatives in Austin. It's the same decision we face in Washington. It needs to be made logically and with commitment. Our lives are controlled by economics as much as they are by ideals. In fact, hard economic times can make weak men ignore values when it comes to putting food on their tables. Yet, in the long run we are all hurt if we sell out to the easy, short-term solutions.

A popular saying in Texas is that "it is far better to teach a man to fish so that he can eat for a lifetime than to give a man a fish in order that he can eat for a day." It sounds simple, but I think it contains the key to strengthening our national economy. It recognizes the fact that government can give free bread to people, or it can create economic opportunity in which we can rely on our own abilities and succeed within the environment we create for ourselves. It also shows how education helps create opportunities for self-sufficiency. That saying has been around Texas for a long time, yet we need to carry it forward as a part of our new legacy of a resolute national will and firm determination to keep our freedoms through judicious economic policies. Economic freedom is directly related to political freedom; the two cannot be separated. If we rely on the state for survival then we are within its control, and our ability to react with independent thought is as limited as if we were existing in a totalitarian state under the threat of martial law. Economic control may be more subtle, but it is equally real. While we recognize and rebel against physical oppression, economic tyranny is tolerated for longer periods of time because it's simply not as obvious. Just as we tend to complain about tax increases, we don't object as much to the far greater amount of money taken from us by tax withholding. We've accommodated to that form of taxation. It is this control over the nature of the economy, the creation of opportunity, or the deprivation of it, that gives government power over our lives. Yet perhaps many of us may not fully recognize this problem.

It is no different than the example of the first Santa Gertrudis Bull Dad bought from the King Ranch to improve his herd. When he released it in our pasture, the bull charged first and then bolted to freedom. It stayed aloof from the herd. I told him that I didn't like the bull, figured he would kill us both, and didn't think he would ever be of use, particularly to a 10-year-old who liked his own freedom in the pasture. But Dad told me to wait. As he continued to feed the cattle, the bull eventually understood that free food was available and made his way to the front to eat out of our hands. This was an effective technique for handling a bull, but it can create problems when we allow it to happen in society. For example, taxation policies can lull us into complacency as we consent to trade current comfort for a loss of independence.

Through government fiscal policy, tremendous amounts of money can be spent on special projects that help either regions or industries. By using taxation policy, government can reward or punish different types of conduct. For example, investment credit encourages industrial development. Increased excise tax on liquor tends to penalize consumption. Through its monetary policy, government can control inflation or deflation, which means that the savings of a lifetime can either be greatly enhanced in real purchasing power or decreased.

Many economic policies affect one another which makes them more complex in combination than they would be by themselves. The fact that our economic policies develop and stay with us over long periods of time makes it more difficult to gain a true perspective on why they were enacted and what benefit, if any, they are providing.

Many policies were created as band-aids to solve short-term problems previous to an election; yet their impact might last for 20 or 30 years. One of the problems in government is that it is easier to get something created, such as an agency or a program in response to an immediate need, than it is to remove the agency or have it discontinued when the need is fulfilled or the policy proves ineffective. Once it is placed in operation, the bureaucracy and the recipients of its largesse become a potent force for maintaining the programs. They may only represent a small number of people who could be even better served by discontinuing the programs; yet they are far more vocal than the majority. As a result, programs often remain even in opposition to the common good of all people, because the people, as a whole, are affected only minutely by the existence of that one program. Only when the people as a whole can see significant benefit can this be overcome as in the federal government's 1986 Tax Reform Act that lumped many of these small items together for discontinuance so that a big enough benefit could be perceived to bring about change.

Our entire economy has been formed through this type of change and gradual adoption of quick-fix policies. More of us are realizing that our federal tax structure is archaic; it is not meeting the needs of our modern world. For example, other countries raise most of their money by value-added taxes which can be rebated to their exporters. Their advantage puts our corporations and businesses which pay corporate income taxes without rebate at a significant disadvantage. Additionally, we reward debt by allowing tax deductions for interest while equity dividends are not deductible. They are often double-taxed. This encourages a large build-up of debt within our economy rather than strengthening injections of equity. Our government policies in agriculture pay people not to plant in order to reduce surpluses. At the same time, government pays for studies to increase production per acre through farm assistance. Other branches provide assistance to undeveloped countries so that they can use our agricultural technology to become self-sufficient. However, we have then replaced our agricultural customers with competitors who do not have the regulatory burdens we have. Government simply has too many activities that are uncoordinated.

Another example of taxation which no longer meets our modern world is the Texas tax structure that has been based on industries, such as petroleum, which have supplied our needs in the past. Now petroleum's production is declining, yet it still bears the major part of the state's tax burden. Many service and technological industries which were not around when the early tax structures were adopted have become significant, and they might be far better able to pay part of the tax burdens.

But the arguments from many of these sectors is that taxes would retard growth, which is particularly important to the economy as a whole. In many cases that argument may be justified, since new industries have relocated to Texas in response to our favorable taxation policies. This creates jobs for Texans, but it doesn't answer the questions of how we fund government. At least in Texas a major effort is being made to follow the recommendation of the House Speaker's Economic Advisory Committee to have a commission that studies the impact of existing and future taxes on Texas and the economy. In my opinion, it is a very positive movement toward a constructive style of government.

In summary, our taxation structures, both in Texas and nationally, have been built over a period of time through reaction to specific short-term needs. They were also created when America was a dominant force in the world economy and did not have to compete with other nations as we do today. Our Texas tax policies were built in a period when we were not looking toward our future as much as we are today. We talk of diversification, which is critically important, but we have not specifically assessed how we will diversify our economy. We talk of high tech and are proud that MCC chose Austin for its headquarters and pioneering work in micro-technology research. But much of the research and development that can provide the additional jobs will be many years in the future, and not all high-tech industries have had a significant growth rate in recent years.

We have in the *interim* the question of what to do with 100,000 to 200,000 workers who were employed by the petrochemical plants on the Gulf Coast and significantly greater numbers in agriculture and the oil industry who are unemployed due to the slump. Those are immediate problems, that can't be solved by jobs ten years in the future.

Agricultural cash flow is another area of substantial change in Texas' economic picture. The Weinstein and Gross study attributes cash flow from agricultural exports to the strong U.S. dollar during 1981–1983. During those three years, the real value of Texas cotton exports declined 48.1 percent. Wheat exports fell by 31.7 percent, and feed grain by 45.8 percent. Other commodities also declined by smaller percentages. Not surprisingly, the poor export performance of these important Texas agricultural products combined with our domestic surpluses has exerted a strong negative influence on our economic well-being. Texas has always been a state closely tied to the land through cattle, cotton, and mineral resources. Thus, the significance of commodity prices is great and can result in large losses if not tempered with other industries which are less susceptible to commodity price swings.

One of the brighter areas in the changing economic picture has been in high technology. Like many other states, Texas has tried to attract high technology concerns. We have been successful as witnessed by the location of MCC in Austin. Companies such as Texas Instruments, Mostek, Motorola, National Semiconductor, and Advanced Micro-Devices have led the way with technological innovation. Yet at the same time, our innovations have been absorbed by foreign competitors who have manufactured products from these new developments at a price below our production costs. Almost 13,000 semiconductor workers were laid off in the Dallas area between 1985 and 1986. A strong dollar and steep competition from abroad have forced companies such as Apple, Xerox, Datapoint, and Data General to reduce production in Texas. The only sector which is still rather strong is the defense-oriented high-tech companies. However, they require computer parts to maintain their operations, and now a majority of these needed resources are controlled by foreign companies.

A new effort between business, education and government leaders has begun to *unify* Texas. Together we are seeking the technology of the future. We have built and will continue to enhance our major medical institutions. We are creating a strong presence in space commercialization and are looking internationally for new frontiers to explore.

The severe economic pressures on the oil and gas, agriculture, and high-tech industrial sectors have affected two other major sectors of our state's economy: real estate and banking. We find in most Texas markets today an abundance of retail, office, and commercial building space available. This multi-year oversupply, coupled with anemic demand, has resulted in record real estate foreclosures and bankruptcy filings.

Likewise, Texas' banking sector has been hit especially hard as commercial borrowers and developers have been unable to generate enough cash flow to make their payments. More bank closings and takeovers have been recorded in recent years than in the previous four decades. Large bank holding companies are analyzing the Texas market, and many smaller banks realize the problems of getting more capital into the state and their communities. Regional banks will have to grow to reach a size sufficient to maintain their independence in the coming interstate national banking trends, if that is their desire.

But Texas banking has more challenges than being gobbled up by large multinational banks. A sophisticated financial system is second, possibly, only to education in rebuilding a strong economy. Few recognize the importance of maintaining a locally-based financial center where decisions will turn on local rather than national considerations. Similarly, few realize how quickly we need to become heavily involved in international finance. Balance has to be found and the question remains whether the balance will come from the weight of lobbyists or intelligent planning.

The interstate banking and branching laws passed by the Texas State Legislature in 1987 have created a new environment in Texas' financial picture. It will take time before that environment is fully developed, but eventually Texas' huge market will be cultivated in a way which will maintain some degree of local control.

Thus, Texas has to become an international trader. At present, we are far from that point. Because of the huge declines in oil property values, real estate, and agriculture, Texas must first get over its liquidity crisis. As the state moves to a gradual diversification of industry, it must reconceptualize its financial networks. Like a human body, there is muscle and blood. One is the industrial base, the other the financial system in which credit circulates. One does not work well without the other. But almost unappreciated by the rest of the world is the fact that Texas is addressing both at a higher level of awareness and sophistication.

It has to be noted that Mexico remains a major influence on the Texas economy. When Mexico prospered, Texas was its partner. When the peso was devalued, our state suffered. The future places great burdens on Mexico's large population, and the United States' Immigration Act which penalizes employers for hiring illegal aliens will effect some sectors of the U.S. economy almost as much as the 1986 Tax Reform Act. The future is uncertain, but it should be noted that Mexico's low labor costs and the "twin plant concept" along the Texas/Mexico border provide lucrative opportunities for Texas to increase its economic edge in international competition. Texas' Hispanic ties, coupled with our universities' emphasis on building cultural, economic, and political appreciation of our southern neighbors, can create opportunities for Texas to become a center of trade and education to Mexico and Central and South America, just as Miami has become the center of the Carribean Basin. Already, the state is moving to enhance that opportunity by working at the personal relationships that are more effective than political ones.

All of these changes—and those mentioned by Weinstein and Gross—have not only drastically affected specific industries, but the ripple effect and loss of cash flow have seriously impacted almost all areas of the state. As of September 1986, more than 900,000 Texans had lost their jobs, and our unemployment rate was at its highest level since the Great Depression. Loss of income reduces our purchasing power which hurts other businesses and merchants. The state and local governments lose revenue from reduced taxes which impacts state employees, teachers, and government-supported programs and services. Weinstein and Gross said this about the loss of 234,000 industrial jobs in Texas during 1986:

". . . wages received by Texas mining and manufacturing workers are comparatively high, with most estimates ranging from $18 to $22 per hour, or roughly $21,500 annually. Thus, the loss of 234,000 industrial jobs in Texas has probably also resulted in the withdrawal of at least

$5 billion in annual payroll and $10.5 billion in annual purchasing power
from the state economy."

Many people in Texas believe that we will rise to these challenges,
and broadened ideas and solutions will be generated. Dr. Weinstein said
in conclusion:

> "Clearly the challenge to Texas in the years ahead will be to wean our-
> selves to the extent possible from these external forces by developing
> our indigenous potential. Future economic development will require a
> set of strategies that is internally as well as externally focused. The
> ultimate goal of these strategies must be to create an economic climate
> that encourages innovation and adaptation and response to the ever-
> changing and increasingly competitive environment that faces Texas."

Texas' economic environment has been a fertile one for small businesses and new business creation. Small, independently-owned and oper-
ated businesses form the backbone of our economy. There are more than
290,000 small, non-farm businesses with fewer than 50 employees in
Texas. This represents 94 percent of the state's businesses. This favorable small business environment is even more important when we realize
that an estimated two-thirds of all new jobs come from businesses em-
ploying fewer than 20 people. The historical attitude of Texans to take
risks is a significant factor. In the east, industry is more developed. Managers rather than entrepreneurs dominate a mature economy. While that
process is occurring in Texas, the desire to be in control of one's own
life rather than be employed by others is still strong, as these figures
indicate.

The feeling of independence people get from financial well-being has
always been a high priority to Texans. But in early Texas, as today, the
form and direction of government had tremendous impact upon the economic system and upon the individual's rights and success under it. *Government, in effect, deals with two broad types of issues: economic issues,
usually in the division and transfer of resources, and moral issues dealing
with crime and punishment.* The moral issues have a great impact upon
the order and degree of security within a society, but the economic issues
have tremendous effect upon how well the society prospers. As we will
see, there are very fundamental differences in the directions that the government can orient a society's economy, and over the longer term these
have great impact upon the standard of living. Natural resources, demographic factors and other considerations can provide benefits, but overall
direction and strategy, usually in the form of tax policy, guides the expec-

tations and allocations of resources within that society. *However, in the future, moral issues will begin to assert a dominance of their own on government that will diminish the focus on economics which is a significant trend and change.*

These trends evolve over longer periods of time and often are not recognized because of the subtle changes they make in a society. The Battle of San Jacinto decisively changed Texas' direction; much as the fate of Europe was settled by Wellington at Waterloo or Charles Martel at Tours. But great moments such as these rarely change history. More often it is perseverance over time that affects the real change in a society and the destiny of a people. Attention must be paid to the ideas that guide a government and lead it to a direction, because in times of great crisis and change, as we have seen in Texas, the direction in which we head and the goal which we seek are critically important.

Perhaps the best example is that while Sam Houston won a great victory at San Jacinto, much of the credit rightfully belonged to Stephen F. Austin. For ten years prior to that victory, Austin had been the negotiator and moderator between two cultures. He bought the time that permitted the Texans to increase in number, in strength, and in unity. Had San Jacinto been fought ten years earlier, there probably would not have been enough Texans to have made a difference. It was Austin's more subtle talents that really brought about the great victory. Few people have read the dreams that he had for Texas. Austin envisioned, in great detail, how the state should develop. He recognized the tremendous importance of education.

The Dictionary of American Biography, Volume I, sets this out very plainly:

> "Austin's conception of his task was expressed in a striking comparison which he made in 1832:
>
>> 'Such an enterprise as the one I undertook in settling an uninhabited country must necessarily pass through three regular gradations. The first step was to overcome the roughness of the wilderness, and may be compared to the labor of the farmer on a piece of ground covered with woods, bushes, and brambles, which must be cut down and cleared away, and the roots grubbed out, before it can be cultivated. The second step was to pave the way for civilization and lay the foundation for lasting productive advancement in wealth, morality, and happiness. This step might be compared to the ploughing, harrowing, and sowing the ground after it is cleared. The third and last and most important step is to give proper and healthy direction to public opinion, morality, and education . . . to give tone, character, and con-

sistency to society, which, to continue the simile, is gathering in the
harvest and applying it to the promotion of human happiness'"

Austin's statements must be viewed as notably farsighted. He knew
where he was going, not only in settling a land, but in trying to build a
society and attempting to move toward a goal. The framers of our national constitution demonstrated the same depth of thought. They sought
not just to write laws that settled differences, not just to argue on individual points, but to create a document that would last.

Government plays a far greater role today in determining the future
of society than it did at the inception of our state or our nation. The policies that now shape our economic future are determined in Austin and in
Washington. As I seek to tell my children what their future is going to be
like, I see great clouds of fog obscuring that vision. Both our state and
our nation face fiscal crises, and we cannot be certain how they are going
to respond. It is easy enough to predict what will happen under certain
circumstances, but the real question lies in the *style of government* that
will be adopted in Austin and in Washington. How will government go
about solving its problems? Will the solutions be the short-term band-
aids often applied in the past? Or will they be well-thought-out, long-
range policies that can help present and future generations remain competitive, thus preserving the standard of living so important to the future
of the family.

Texas is a perfect place to start. The state faces a severe budget
crisis at a time when conditions in its prison system require massive
funding. Most Texans oppose raising taxes, but a great need exists for
additional funds in education, economic development, and social welfare.
The legislature must prioritize and address these problems. In the realm
of politics, the legislators simply place bills in the hopper to solve individual needs. While there are numerable ideas for dealing with the problems
the state faces, a time of crisis offers special opportunities. Appropriate
solutions can be focused on the common good.

Budgetary battles are not just contests to balance numbers, instead
they represent a struggle to determine government's proper role in society. The manner in which the government solves its problems will have
tremendous ramifications for each of us. Too often, the response to a crisis is like a shotgun blast—much noise and many pellets sprayed in a
broad direction that accomplishes little, because the target is too far
away. Government's real success comes when it can unify to the extent
that it sees a vision of where it wants to be for the future—much like the
early Texans and the framers of the constitution. Only a bullet from a

carefully aimed rifle can be expected to travel any distance with accuracy. Some say this cannot be done in modern politics, because people are not patient. But I feel that people, particularly Texans, are willing to sacrifice, if they feel the ideals are worthy enough and the strategy sufficiently intelligent.

Texas House Speaker Gib Lewis' Economic Development Committee was carefully selected to pull together broad-range thinkers to focus, not just on the immediate crisis, but on the future of the state as well. It brought a greater depth of macro economics and considerations to his staff than normally would be found in Austin politics. That became important, because economic development was the key issue that could affect all other state problems. *Unlike the concepts of "no new taxes" or "compassion", long-term enhancement of people's standard of living is a philosophy of government's role.* It helps balance concern between taxation and compassion and deals with the actual purpose of government around which we can coordinate policy. It also helps define the relationship between the state and society. When the crisis is particularly difficult, you often can't find a good short-term solution, and you must look long-range. *Government is not a zero sum equation of more taxes or less spending, good policy matters because the system is dynamic not static.*

In Texas, economic development is now concentrated in a new Texas Department of Commerce charged with recruiting new business and industries. That might provide short-term benefits by presenting the state in the best light—much like putting a new coat of paint on an old tractor to make it sell better. But the real value of that tractor would be whether or not it runs well and what it can actually produce.

Therefore, if government's efforts are to be truly effective, economic development needs to be viewed from a long-term perspective. It involves the state's governmental policies, and educational systems that foster not only research and development, but more importantly, a technologically adaptable work force to fill higher paying jobs in the future. Those considerations directly affect budgets in the form of taxes, education, and quality of life.

Structuring government policy on economic development can be likened to arranging dominoes from a pile into a straight line. The direction is critical. The first domino chosen has a great effect on the entire circle of options. A simple example would be the strategy by which one constructs a policy. Philosophers have always noted that there are many answers, but the important point is identifying the basic question. There has been a trend in Texas to let the government do only what the private sector could not do. Rather than create new agencies to promote Texas, state government can coordinate regional and local chambers of commerce, industrial foundations, and urban industrial development groups. Those groups already have expertise, but it needs to be blended and used more effectively. Money would be better spent by coordinating the private sector rather than creating grant programs or government work projects. By serving as a coordinator, government could assist the private sector in concentrating its efforts in a positive direction. This approach could actually change government rather than leaving it mired in indecision.

I think most of what Texas government could do for its economy is more a matter of image than substance. The United States and other nations may hold back their investment dollars while trying to determine whether Texas is commited to participation in a modern world through educational funding, long-term economic development and emergence as the "third coast of thought" for an enlightened capitalism. If Texas pulls back in a reactionary fashion by cutting all costs, particularly if that is done in a parochial and partisan way, this state's future will be dim. Thus, the world's perception of Texas is critically important to its economy and future. Texas is currently in the bottom of an economic cycle, from which it will inevitably emerge because it is a strong market. But in the interim, perceptions of Texas can greatly impact our recovery speed and future growth rate. In effect, the rest of the world looks to the *style* of government in Texas, because it represents the judgment of Texans in choosing their leaders. Taxes are important, and they must be restrained to the greatest degree possible. However, they do not operate in a vacuum, and we can analyze whether they constitute an expense or investment. If it is an expense, is it wasteful or critical? *An investment can be judged on whether it fits into an overall plan so that it can be compared to other options, but you must have a plan in order to judge.*

For that reason, one of the major recommendations by the Speaker's Advisory Committee was not that he support an individual bill, but that he form a commission of 24 members, involving the Governor as Chairman, the Lieutenant Governor, the Speaker and the heads of all of the various agencies which could affect future economic development, be it through education, agriculture or the legislative process. This commission would form a united body to look at the direction in which long-term policy should move, and which would have the *combined political power and understanding* to commit the state's resources. Government needs to be responsive to the grassroots concerns of citizens. I believe the best way to represent those interests is to have a discerning and coordinated policy orchestrated at the highest level of government. *Power operates most effectively when it is directed downward from the top. Many issues rise from the bottom, but they are uncoordinated and can stall the process of crisis control by creating delays and political problems.*

A potent force can be created within a government from a bi-partisan commitment to a sound strategy. Government reacts to the powers wielded by key leaders and seldom operates in any other fashion. Some would say that it is difficult for four or five key leaders to agree on a single policy, but that is not necessarily the case. Governor Bill Clements appointed a separate committee whose recommendations closely paralleled those of the Speaker's Advisory group. The difficulty comes in pulling government together and using the equivalent of a scientific method to develop and direct a policy.

Too often, each individual in government—and that individual's staff, no matter how honorable these people may be—has his own agenda and approach. And more than anything else, the fear in government is making the wrong decisions, because so many people are uninformed and often do not consider issues with much depth or logic. The population generally votes its short-term pocketbook, and that says a great deal to those who would invest in the state.

Many ideas being recommended in Texas, from the deregulation of intra-state commerce to capital formation programs, second lien mortgages, improved quality of public education, increased research and development funding, business incubators, and even expanded taxes, are all secondary to a coordinated philosophy. An excellent expression of perspective says that a man on top of a mountain and a man at the bottom of a mountain each have a different opinion of whether the path between them goes up or down. If you were to bring the two back a distance and let them look at the mountain from afar, they would realize simply that the path goes both ways. For an effective style of government, our leaders need to pull back to get a perspective on economic growth. They need to concern themselves with the future standard of living of our people, and not let just short-term considerations affect their choices. They need to realize that new ideas and radical concepts are important in times of crisis, when tremendous change has taken place and past approaches are no longer acceptable.

Government has limited margin for error in these difficult times. It must adopt a style that seeks to accomplish the most with the least use of resources. Too often, the politics of Austin produces individuals who assume office and personalize that office for themselves. They should realize that though they are individually important, what they accomplish for the state is their true legacy. This can be best achieved by remembering what their principles were when they entered office, rather than letting the trappings of power and the press releases of their staff make them hesitant to broaden their viewpoints and ideas.

Texas needs to adopt a vision in its style of government that does not try to copy Massachussetts and North Carolina, for if we are 20 years behind them now—and they continue moving forward—we will remain 20 years behind. We need to project much further ahead on the curve to become the international traders that we are capable of being. We need to adapt our education to prepare us for that future. If we can once find that vision, which I feel exists now among the most knowledgeable leaders of our state, then we must agree on the proper allocation of resources.

My father used the common sense approach, or the rusty pipe theory, to describe the allocation of government resources. Dad was a fairly staunch fiscal conservative, but he also was a visionary who knew the importance of growth. To him, this was not at all inconsistent. The allocation of resources was judged largely by whether it was an investment or an expenditure. It was not necessarily a liberal or conservative issue as much as it was a question of cost benefit for the long-term. He used to say that if a liberal spender looked at a rusted pipe, he would immediately want to replace it with a new one. If a reactionary spender looked at it, he would want to put on a coat of paint and not spend the money for the new pipe, but at least try to make it look good. To Dad, the conservative approach was somewhere in between. He thought you should sand all the rust off the pipe, because a paint job on the rust would flake off quickly and allow the deterioration to continue. If, after you had evaluated the situation, the pipe was weak, you bought a new one. If the pipe looked strong enough, you painted it and made do with the least expense. One should always be skeptical, but not negativist; there is a big distinction.

The question was not one of policy, but one of considering each alternative and then arriving at the best solution. He felt you had to blend compassion and fiscal responsibility. Government does have a role, and normally it is to do those things the private sector can't do, but what should be done if you are to have an ethical society which meets the society's true needs.

But the problem that Dad noted, and that I notice even more today, is that politicians tend to look at issues with more emotion than thought. They ask people how they feel rather than what they think. They seldom look at the implications of individual issues in the overall scope of what government should do and what it should not do. They talk about the dollars involved more than whether the government should be involved at all. And too often they look at issues from an extreme point of view.

Perhaps no issue will so greatly affect Texas nor be discussed more in the coming decade than the commitment of funds to education. Everyone understands that the technological future requires a major commitment not only to the research and development of our higher education institutions, but also in the commitment to public education. The population can then better adapt to the higher paying job-needs of new technological development. The standard of living, so important to us individually and to our families, will rest on the quality of our jobs—and that will depend on our capability to produce in a competitive world.

This means we must make major commitments to education, but at the same time, we cannot afford to have a high tax rate that pulls large amounts of money from the private sector, where it is most productive, into the governmental sectors where often it is not as well spent. To many, the argument is better education with higher taxes or less education with lower taxes. Neither is an acceptable choice nor the correct one. We have to be commited to education but like Dad's rusted pipe theory, we need to look at the situation more closely. We have abundant resources; 53 percent of our budget in the state of Texas is commited to education, yet there is a difference between allocating money to education and the administration of those funds. Recently, newspaper articles showed a large amount of funding for additional classrooms for one of the state's institutions, but noted that there had been significant objections because the classrooms that presently existed were utilized only 30 percent of the time.

Unquestionably, to get the most out of education, we need to see that money effectively used. If the political strength exists to manage those funds for the highest and best use, we could maintain our tax basis and greatly enhance our educational system as well. The problem is that many educators are not as familiar with normal business practices and the needs of the outside business community as they might believe. Similarly, in the legislature, there is limited understanding of the complexities of the universities and the intense competition to attract top quality faculty members. Both the legislature, which wishes to balance its budget without taxes, and the university and school administrators, who understandably fight for the highest funding that they can obtain, defend their own viewpoints—oftentimes in excess. *There needs to be a partnership, a common area of interest that has not existed, but that must be fostered in this difficult period.* It is far from impossible, because in times of crisis groups have unified in the past to accomplish a common end. Education is no different from the rest of the bureaucracies within state government, and the people of Texas should hold all parties accountable.

Administrators must understand that people are highly sensitive to the ploy administrations use in closing libraries on Sunday to send a message home that education needs funding, while at the same time they may be spending large sums on underutilized facilities. This is similar to the tactic practiced in other states for cutting back highway funds. The bureaucratic strategy was to fill no potholes and discontinue needed maintenance in order to seed public discontent, even though there were other areas that could have been cut more easily with less effect on the public. That type of approach can be counteracted by leaders coming forward with ideas that will convince people that change is necessary, and these are the most intelligent choices available. This is possible only when personal political considerations are put aside and the entire leadership of a state stands firmly united.

That sense of commitment can be conveyed to the media and the people, and it can create a perception of Texas as a state with vision and resolve. It is my sincere hope that this is the direction Texas leadership will take over the next few years, as these critical policies are determined and affect future generations. Policies must be coordinated; they must be unified; and they must reflect a visionary understanding of government's role in relation to society.

As we speak of Texas' economic future, I feel relatively certain we will see the new and expanded Texas Department of Commerce incorporate many of the recommendations of the Texas Research League Report that was prepared for the Speaker of the Texas House as part of his economic development approach. But the key thing for each of us to know is that no matter how well-planned and thought-out any piece of legislation appears on paper, it has many of the characteristics of a beautiful rifle. It looks impressive, but the telling questions are: "Is it loaded?" "Is it capable of shooting?" "Who is aiming it?" And, "At what?" Any policy and public pronouncement can lull the public into believing that a solution is taking place. But only commitment and vision can make an idea, the basis of government policy, into a reality. And what we in Texas and this nation must never forget is that those government policies we so often take for granted will affect our future and that of our children.

In chemistry, certain reactions occur or speed up because of the presence of another component. The product isn't effective if the catalyst isn't present. In our public policy, particularly in economics, I feel that education works as a catalyst. In the 1970s, our escalating wealth was spent freely, making Texas a place of economic growth and increased influence. This wealth and influence, combined with a spirit of state pride, inspired us to believe that, with a renewed vigor, we could accomplish whatever goals we set. If our minds could conceive it, Texans could do it.

As a result of this buoyant feeling, Texas leaders began looking at what we needed as a state to achieve our potential. Education was one of the top items. Former Governor Allan Shivers was chairman of the Board of Regents of the University of Texas system during this time, and he invited many of Texas' young leaders to participate in an analysis of the state's future. Shivers was a man who had traveled extensively and participated in decision-making circles throughout the world. He guided us in understanding that our state would be judged not just by its wealth and political power, but by its intelligence and culture as well. Governor Shivers had the foresight to see that our state's real future resource was its people. If we were to understand the economic, political, and moral changes which were on the horizon, he knew that we'd have to be an educated society. He explained that Texas' wealth would have to be used with wisdom, foresight and a broadened perspective. In Governor Shiver's mind, building an excellent university would be one of the best uses of that wealth.

This was not a new idea. From the time of the Republic, Texans have been committed to education. Millions of acres of West Texas land were granted to the University of Texas system to build a first-class university. The system now has campuses in all parts of the state, but the bulk of the permanent university fund went to the University of Texas at Austin and to Texas A&M University in College Station. Over the years there were repeated challenges to take this money that had been earmarked for building educational excellence and use it for other purposes or split it among other institutions.

Two theories, each with intelligent proponents, were set forth about how the funds should be used. One position held that the money was for education and could best be spent by spreading it over many universities and campuses, so that all of them would be improved to some degree. Governor Shivers and former University of Texas System Chancellor Charles LeMaistre held the other theory: that we needed certain universities to stand above all others, and that we should concentrate funds to build the best rather than spreading the money so thinly that no institution would have an opportunity to achieve outstanding excellence. A typical example of the issues at stake concerned college libraries. Assuming the libraries had an adequate base of books, the question arose whether it was better to add a number of the same books to a number of college libraries or create one outstanding research-oriented library at which the best minds could study. The questions were complex, and everyone realized there was justice in both viewpoints. In the end, however, many of those who analyzed the issue concurred on the priority of building for excellence rather than quantity.

At that point, people began to share Governor Shiver's perspective on why an outstanding university was so important to Texas. It provided a foundation for what we could become and how other states and countries would regard us. Both the governor and my Dad believed that education affected a society more than any other force: if we want to be the best, we have to learn from the best. As even greater oil wealth flowed into Texas, other state schools continued to criticize the allotment of money to the University of Texas and Texas A&M. The chief complaint was that these universities were trying to buy credibility by hiring the best professors. Whenever I heard those criticisms I couldn't help but smile, because it appeared that Texans were using their money to build a future based on intelligence. We were spending our money wisely. Competition always hurts, and Texas was finally competing in the world market for intelligence.

Now that state budgets are tight and oil prices are down, our Legislature is looking at ways to let the universities conduct their research in joint ventures with private industry. This not only helps the budgets, but it encourages the best minds to cooperate and benefit personally in the profits. Texans don't like paying taxes or being second best, so ingenuity in government has become a necessity. But the debate about funding for higher education has only started. It represents a huge component of the state budget. Combined with funding for primary education, these two levels of education compose 53 percent of Texas' total budget. Major structural reforms to cut costs will be suggested while others argue for more money. A task force has studied the issue, and the resolution of these choices on education may well set the stage for the issue of economic development, because the two are so intertwined.

In relation to this, we need to understand educational reform in Texas. We have been working for many years on improving our educational system. If you were in Texas when the sweeping educational reform bill was passed in 1984, you had the benefit of seeing public policy being made. There was a lot of heated debate for and against the bill. Many parents lined up against one part of the package that said if students don't pass their academic subjects, they will not be allowed to engage in any extracurricular activities for a period of six weeks.

After a long hiatus from the basics of reading, writing, and arithmetic, public school education was being revitalized. Ross Perot, then chairman and chief executive officer of Electronic Data Systems in Dallas, was put in charge of discovering ways in which Texas public schools could be improved. He spent nine months away from his company and held hearings around the state listening to teachers, administrators, and parents give testimony and offer solutions to the educational challenges we faced. Rarely had we seen the entire state mobilized to address an issue. People took the time to make their ideas heard. Many of us called and wrote to our senators and legislators, and others walked the halls of our state capitol to lobby for their viewpoint. The elected State School Board was dismissed, and the Governor appointed new members.

Because agriculture and oil have dominated the state's economy, Texans have been dismissed by some people as non-intellectual. We dealt with tangibles such as oil, cattle, and crops rather than intellectual products. We have not built a large venture capital industry, nor fully appreciated high technology. Our congressmen and senators were told to secure military bases, not research facilities. Thus some of the perception of Texas being behind the intellectual/educational curve may have been true in the past, but it is not necessarily accurate for the future. Texas, particularly its leadership, has always had great respect for education. Large amounts of land and resources have been set aside for educational goals. Texans may have to re-orient their direction and concentration of resources in education because of the current economic conditions. Just throwing money at education has never been an answer. Administrators may confuse spending money with educational benefit. The two are not the same and examples of administrative waste and incompetence should not detract from our appreciation for the value of quality education. We must learn more about refining the educational system, rather than commit only to broad concepts of education. It will be a hard-earned battle.

One of the most difficult challenges, other than fighting for education, will be reaching a decision about increased taxes and increasing government involvement in the private sector. The lack of corporate or personal income tax in Texas has provided our citizens with an abundance of jobs. This has been the major reason for our growth and a significant example of the benefits of limited government interference in the private sector. Unfortunately, it is going to be increasingly difficult to attract jobs, if we have to impose major taxes upon the business sector. Businesses have the opportunity to relocate in many other states or foreign countries where labor is inexpensive. Each time legislators think about taxing a business, they believe they are avoiding taxes for their constituency, the consumers. In the early stages that may appear to be good political philosophy, but in the long run the constituents will be hurt. Businesses respond to the lowest cost of production. This is necessary because of competition. We need to be as concerned with the total tax load. Today our heavy property taxes are more feared by business than an equal amount of corporate income tax which would decrease in bad years.

Business is not an adversary of the common man. In fact, today in America, business to a great degree personifies the common man. When a business fails, individual people are hurt. A large percentage of a company's income is paid to its employees, and a much smaller portion to shareholders in the form of dividends. In many cases, the stock is held not by wealthy individuals, but by pension funds and insurance companies that represent the savings of millions of Americans who work or did work and are now retired. If the insurance company's rates are good, then the dividends on an individual's policies increase, his pension fund grows more rapidly, and his job is secure. But if the business fails, he loses his job, his investments decline in value and other taxpayers may have to support him through unemployment compensation and other benefit programs. If the banks and savings & loans that provide money to these companies fail or incur large losses, this affects the soundness of our system and the expansiveness and aggressiveness with which the financial organizations can encourage new growth. And of equal importance, the government loses a taxpayer who shares the burden at many levels.

Thus, the economic system is interconnected, just like the human body. If a thorn lodges in our foot, our entire body is uncomfortable until it is removed. Our economy functions in the same way; for every action there is a reaction. Normally the reactions take place in the form of government policies, but it is important to realize that those policies cause reactions in their own right. Policies intended as short-term fixes may cause long-term reactions.

An example of cause and effect in our economic system can be seen in the costly but largely ineffective social programs of the 1960s and 1970s. Many members of Congress and state legislatures believed that America could help people by taxing businesses and wealthy individuals heavily and distributing that money to economically poor families. We demonstrated compassion to assist those who were less fortunate. The problem was not in our motivation. The difficulty was the methods we used in trying to accomplish our good intentions of increasing the economic well-being of all our citizens.

Building a solid economic base for all Americans begins with wise policies and requires a basic understanding of the two ways in which government raises money. It can tax, which is usually unpopular, or it can inflate the currency—in effect, print more money—which reduces the value of debt and is a form of debt liquidation. In economics, there is a general relationship that simplifies the concept called the quantitative theory of money. It is expressed in an equation form (price = money supply/ amount of goods). Generally speaking, if the supply of money rises faster than the supply of available goods, prices rise and inflation results.

Because of the great spending programs and the reluctance to impose taxation during Vietnam and the latter stages of the Great Society, America effectively monetized debt by issuing substantial amounts of government obligations and increasing the money supply. In substance, that was one of the causes for inflation in the late 1970s. The increase in oil prices additionally created one of the most difficult inflation situations the nation had seen in modern times. This resulted in a policy reversal in 1979, when the Federal Reserve allowed interest rates to seek their own level. Emphasis was placed on limiting the increase in growth of the money supply rather than controlling interest rates themselves. While these theories are detailed even for economists, they are worthy of anyone's additional study and thoughts.

Our Federal deficits are a major concern. Increased taxes can reduce them, or inflation can make them appear to be less costly because they are paid back in cheaper dollars. This latter approach is far more common in less developed countries. We will have serious policy choices, if we have a confidence crisis where we cannot simply postpone the issue by continued borrowing. The fact that we now are a debtor nation brings this day of reckoning much closer. International markets will soon become saturated with our debt.

For that reason many of the programs that contributed to inflation were intended to help the poor and unfortunate. The inflation that resulted in part from some governmental policies is a form of taxation because it benefits debtor groups at the expense of creditor groups in the short-run. But inflation distorts the allocation of financial resources and necessitates an ultimate adjustment that can be painful to the nation's working force. Inflation, as experienced by economically underprivileged people, brought tremendous increases in the costs of food, transportation, rents, and other necessities of life. These people had no property which increased in value from inflation.

So the real burden of the government policies did not fall upon those whom the lawmakers were targeting. In the long run, the burden fell upon poor people. Lawmakers, however, who could tell their constituencies that they had done a great amount of good for them, received loyal support. While few people understood the long-term consequences of public policies on economics, most politicians realized that point very well and used it to enhance their prestige. Deflation normally has been harder on the wealthy, who often leveraged to take advantage of tax policy and who owned resources which declined in value. Thus, the effects of directional changes in price level often affect segments of the population differently.

The world has been filled with examples of well-intentioned government policy causing or aggravating economic difficulty. The consequences of the Great Depression were intensified considerably by government policy. If we look at Ethiopia, much of the starvation results not just from the drought, but also from unwise governmental policies. Those policies affect market prices and distribution of products that cause economic dislocations. Thus governments commit sins of both commission and omission. Constructive policies can promote agricultural development through intelligent agricultural education. Rather than feeding people for several days, government and well-intentioned citizens can fight hunger more efficiently by helping people get back on their feet, while finding positive ways to develop these economies for long-term health and prosperity.

Government and economy are thus completely entwined today. This may be substantially more so in underdeveloped countries where, for political stability, the government often has to push growth rates in an attempt to raise the standard of living as a means of dealing with public unrest. The Sicartsa Steel Facility in Mexico is an example. The Mexican government's economic strategy had promoted private economic expansion by protecting industry and by building such essentials as roads, bridges and airports. However, the Mexican economy wasn't growing fast enough in the early 1970s to employ the youth of that nation. Mexico decided to hit the economic accelerator by investing directly in heavy industry. Construction was begun on the steel plant in the '70s, and the government spent billions of dollars of public money. But international steel competition has made it questionable whether the facility can be finished, and if so whether it will ever make money. Originally, it was a project to help the workers, create jobs, and increase their standard of living. Now it is a drain upon the Mexican people, with the potential of producing exatly the opposite effect.

When creating solutions and building a strong national will in economics, our policymakers need to consider long-range effects and benefits; they also must be consistent and adhere to sound principles. Policies need to be based upon intelligent and thoughtful long-term goals, not immediate band-aid solutions of more help to political careers than the country.

The American people, on the whole, have less understanding of government's impact upon our standard of living than do people of many under-developed countries. Those people have seen how government inter-ference with business produces negative effects on their personal lives within a short period of time. In many countries, an increase in the money supply is followed quickly by inflation, and cutbacks or expansions in a government's fiscal programs have an even more immediate effect. If you travelled to the Caribbean nations or France at the time our dollar was weak, you noticed a great difference in people's readiness to accept dollars and what they were willing to pay for them. Not so in the United States, where, because of its size, stability, and international position, economic policies generally bear fruit some years after actions have been taken.

America has been a dominant country with great margin for eco-nomic ups and downs. As a result, we have not suffered serious depres-sions as we did in the past. But the 40 years of economic dominance are ending. It is not that the United States is particularly declining, it is that the rest of the world has caught up with us. At the end of World War II, all of our industries were working at almost peak capacity, because we were the productive engine of our allies. Much of Japan's economy was in shambles. Heavy bombing in Europe had devastated many other coun-tries. The atomic bomb had given us a nuclear superiority which allowed us to divert our resources to help our own people. Following World War II, we were interested in satisfying American's housing demands. The war had interrupted life for approximately five to six years; new families were being formed, and life was returning to normal. We longed for comfort and routine as quickly as possible, and we wanted to remain safely within our borders to pursue the American Dream. America began buying houses on controlled interest rates, and the economy boomed.

But in more recent times, we have been affected by a rising *world* economy. The American government could more or less dictate the in-terest rates that were paid on savings to match whatever policies it par-ticularly wished to promote, which often were related to the strength of the lobbies within Washington and the special interests. However, when the rest of the world started paying more interest on deposits, we began to see sophisticated money move out of the United States. Generally, in-terest rate is related to risk. If the risks are the same, and one interest rate is regulated and another is higher because it is not, by the nature of the free market system it is likely that money will move to the other location.

Democracy does not have exchange controls and allows money to move freely. As a result, American capital began to drain out of our own national system, and we were forced to pay more competitive interest rates and move into the international arena. In the United States, money market funds could invest in obligations which allowed them to pay higher interest than the banks, since the funds were not regulated by the banking laws. Large amounts of money moved by disintermediation from savings & loans and banks into mutual funds. This resulted in the deregulation of the banking industry, which allowed banks to compete for depositors' money.

This reversed the existing trend because now high interest rates were being paid for savings, thereby necessitating much higher rates for home borrowers or other business borrowers. The banks needed not only to make the normal margin for profit and overhead, but additionally, had to add in an inflation premium, because the dollars that they would get back would be worth less than those that they lent. The American system, unlike the British and other systems, has forced American banks to stay strictly within the banking business. Many major banks throughout the world are, in effect, merchant banks that can become involved in commerce themselves. The holding company acts that have been enacted in the recent times have been moving in this direction. It is a natural consequence brought about not only by the direct desires of the banks for growth, but by their necessity to be placed in a competitive position in an international market. Nonetheless, the restrictions on our large banks have limited their growth, and they are falling rapidly behind other international banks in size. Finance is the lifeblood of industry, and this does not speak well for our vision or future based on present policies.

The point is that times have changed; the past is no longer going to be the guide for the future in economics, and it is absolutely essential to recognize that in setting policies. To return to the past is like being nostalgic for the cavalry when you are fighting tanks. We have to understand the present world reality plus the changes occurring within it. We also need to comprehend the transitions taking place within our economy. Then we'll have a better understanding about the policies that can be put into effect to insure long-term stable growth. Many people predict that America will simply decline and Texas will never recover, since oil can be produced internationally by desperate sellers; but that doesn't necessarily take past history into consideration.

While economic history is the story of one nation overtaking another, it is also the story of the resourcefulness of people. After World War II, it was said that Japan would have to rely on the charity of its neighbors and would never truly recover. Today, it is becoming the dominant economic force—an economic super power in its own right. Argentina had vast amounts of natural resources 20 years ago and based on forward projections, should have become a powerful emerging nation. However, governmental policies took it in an entirely different direction.

The pace of change is affecting almost every nation, and the faster change occurs, the more noticeable its impact on people. Throughout history, two things—increased speed in transportation and communication—have brought people and nations closer together. Technology has leap-frogged in both of these areas, escalating changes in our lifestyles as our world effectively grows smaller. Over the next 20 years internationalization will gain momentum through declines in communication and transportation costs and export and import policies.

The practice of arbitrage will be another contributing factor to the growth of internationalism. In financial arbitrage, some interest rates or currency exchanges are undervalued, while others are overvalued. The concept of arbitrage is not different from water seeking its own level—it simply applies to money. When there is an imbalance between two values, someone tries to profit from that imbalance. If labor is extremely cheap in Indonesia or Korea, and an item can be made there at one-tenth the cost of producing it in the United States, some company will either move to those countries or import a product incorporating that cost difference. This lowers the cost within the market and permits the seller to undercut his competition, thereby getting a greater market share.

If a contractor is bidding on a construction project, he will use the lowest-cost steel in order to get the job. If he can buy steel at under-market prices outside the United States, he probably will use that less-expensive source. It is in his self-interest, and it also serves the self-interest of the American consumer. What everyone desires is an increased standard of living. We want to buy more for our money. The cheaper the production costs of items we purchase, the better our standard of living will be, because we'll have more money to spend on other products.

Entrepreneurs from many different nations will introduce technology and capital into poorer countries in order to raise productivity and income. This will tend to hold down wages and prices in the richer developed countries. As we noted previously, the impact of communication technology can be seen in processing items such as airline tickets. After being collected, airline tickets can be shipped to the Caribbean where, at low labor costs, they can be fed mechanically into an electronic network that sends information back by satellite to the United States. The process is far cheaper than if it were done in the United States. Jobs are created within the Caribbean while jobs are lost in the United States. The same is true relative to the purchase of foreign steel or computer chips.

There is also an increasing internationalization of equity ownership in companies. Americans own companies throughout the world, just as other foreign investors and countries own a large part of America because of the stability of its economic and political environment. It is significant, however, to note that America, for the first time in many years, has now become a debtor nation—a stark example of the trend we have just discussed. Other countries will be heavily investing their surplus dollars here because of our state system and large market. The decreasing value of the dollar in comparison to many currencies makes investing in America a bargain. This is not bad, since they purchase our debt; but in time we will lose our autonomous control. It is important to remember they will repatriate their profits as we always have.

The question is how will America react to this challenge. In the past, societies attempted to cope with such adjustments in two basic ways. One is currency devaluation. The other is protectionism. Heavy taxes and tariffs are placed upon foreign products to equate their costs with normal American production. This may save American jobs temporarily, and it may be a political method for controlling our national economy. Unfortunately, internationalization tends to destroy the concept of an internal national economy and puts us within a world economy. Consequently, international trade and economic considerations prevent political policies from being formed by our own government. If interest rates are 6 percent inside the U.S. and 10 percent in other nations, the only thing the government can do is enforce foreign exchange controls to keep money within our borders. That can have the same effect as rent controls. Eventually controls lead to long-term deterioration of the investment environment and job markets. Because of self-interest, people invest where the benefits are greatest to them, and they react negatively to government interference.

We must realize that our standard of living is going to be heavily influenced by international competition which pulls prices down and reduces domestic inflation. It lowers prices for consumers, because products are produced at the lowest cost. If we want to buy a belt that can be made for $1 in Mexico, but costs $3 to be produced in the United States, do we want to pay the $3? Traditionally, our answer has been, "No." We could allow government to restrict our choices by force, but free trade is an important part of our definition of liberty.

Many times we see instances of unfairness when a foreign government subsidizes the production of an item which is dumped in the United States at below an industry's cost. The United States has regulations to oppose this type of market abuse. Sometimes the regulations have not been as effective as we would desire. However, there is a narrow line between fair trade and free trade. We want to preserve unencumbered trade without tariff barriers while maintaining an atmosphere of fairness.

Economic growth moved from Europe to America, and now it is beginning to move to the Pacific Rim and Japan. In the future that growth will probably move to countries like Korea, China, India, and South American nations such as Brazil. If we ask what promotes decline as societies mature, we'll generally find the same causes that affected America: a lack of basic drive and entrepreneurial spirit as well as changing economic and political conditions. Natural resources have not been the prime motivator of change, because Japan had almost none. That country was almost destroyed after World War II. Yet the Japanese relied on education, sending their students abroad to study the latest technological advances to rebuild their industries. They built a system on cooperation between labor, business, and government that works. But their population's median age is higher than ours, and the dollar's decline has had a major impact on Japan. We often look only at our own problems yet we have to realize that the natural laws of economics can hinder our competition as well. We can build a productive and strong future, but that requires realism, vision and properly executed policies. How wise we are in establishing a new trade policy and the approach we will take on other issues will say much about the depth of our wisdom. It is a pressing issue that will force resolution.

In his book, *The Next Economy,* Paul Hawken tells us about the transitional stage in which Texans and all people within this country find themselves. Hawken says that we are moving from a mass economy, characterized by large consumption of "raw materials, energy, and embodied resources" needed to produce a product, to an informational society in which products are still produced, but with more conservative use of raw materials, energy, and human labor. He does not say that the evolving economy is inherently superior to the mass economy. It is simply different and will require a different attitude. In his own words, Hawken says:

> "The information economy is characterized by people producing and consuming smaller numbers of goods that contain more information. What is this information? It is design, utility, craft, durability, and knowledge added to mass. It is that quality and intelligence that makes a product more useful and functional, longer-lasting, easier to repair, lighter, stronger, and less consumptive of energy."

The very object of production is to produce an acceptable product at the lowest possible cost. For that reason, it is significant that labor costs in many underdeveloped countries are substantially less than those of the

United States, giving others a competitive advantage. However, if the United States makes changes in our method of producing products, we can regain our competitive edge. If we use robots in manufacturing, as is presently being done in a number of heavy industries, precision can be perfect, repetition automatic and labor costs substantially reduced. As computer chips put tremendous amounts of information in very small areas, we can have intensely better-quality items ranging from self-regulating thermostats to talking toys.

The answer to the international competition of the future lies in staying ahead in the changing economy. Americans have always been pioneers. We often suffer some reversals—proving the old adage that every pioneer can be recognized by the arrows in his back, but leadership also carries with it distinct advantages. The problem today is that our research and development are declining. Our educational systems are based on the desires of our students, who often don't focus on the needed job specialties as directly as some of our competitors. Most importantly, our competitors have not only caught up to us, but they are now becoming our equal in many fields and attaining leadership in others.

Many experts are concerned that America's heavy industrial sector, which is actually the productive sector of our economy, is becoming a small percentage of our gross national product. Service industries such as finance, real estate, and other financial rather than industrial businesses do not actually produce salable products. Some people read this as a weakening of the American economy, because they feel that we have less productive capacity than we had in the past to meet international competition. In some ways, this may be an accurate observation, but it is not the whole picture. When we were in the agricultural era, it took a great deal more time to produce the same amount of food than it does today with heavy equipment, fertilizers, and specialized knowledge. Although the number of farmers and amount of required farming hours shrank, we did not necessarily produce less. We only produced it more intelligently, and in most cases, it was less expensive.

The same may be true of the technological revolution, as I have discovered in bank consulting. Knowledge of how specific volumes of transactions can be related to productivity and used as a judgment factor for staffing and planning should have been in operation all along, particularly in cost accounting industries. However, it was not a necessity, because banks had been regulated. Regulation Q told banks what they could pay, and usury ceilings told them what they could charge. Banks' main goals had been growth-oriented until the impact of competitive deregulation hit them. The analysis of volume to productivity makes money for everyone involved. The bank gains, because it can reduce costs. Consultants performing such analyses prosper, because they receive fees. Customers gain, because service charges can be lowered (or not increased) if productivity saves cost. Workers benefit because it keeps their companies strong and profitable. This concept needs to be implemented within government and education.

However, as this begins to take place, and we see the American economy change, we need to recognize some very important characteristics that are changing within it. Not only is our industrial base evolving from a mass production to an information society; not only are we facing an international economy that will be extremely competitive for both American jobs and American products; but our financial system is also undergoing widespread changes. Finance is the lifeblood of commerce, and even though we are trying to make a transition within our economy to lower taxes, more growth, deregulation, and free enterprise, we face a major hurdle from the past. The consequences of our past excesses are increasing debt and leverage; these are our largest challenges. Debt can be reflected in terms of growing amounts of dollars. In contrast, leverage is a factor of degree. I look at it as the relationship of percentage of debt to net worth. Pure debt is not necessarily good or bad. In certain circumstances, leverage can be extremely helpful, because it can increase returns dramatically. In other cases, it can be disastrous, because it adds to a fall as quickly as it does to a rise.

Consider for example, people who had a $40,000 mortgage on a $50,000 house in the late 1960s. They felt fairly heavily leveraged at 80 percent, if that was their only major asset. But if they could make the payments, it was a very manageable debt. Over a decade, with inflation, the house may have doubled in value to $100,000, and perhaps the remaining debt was somewhere around $35,000. Even though there was not much decrease in the amount of debt because of the long-term payout, homeowners certainly felt there was a tremendous decrease in the amount of leverage, because their equity had increased.

They now had a cushion between the fair market value of the house and what they owed on it—or a value of three times that debt. In effect, inflation had decreased their leverage, and they had profited greatly by having the debt, since their return on equity in buying the house was very substantial.

Feeling wealthy, the homeowners in our example decided to increase their standard of living by making a number of additions to the house. They could still handle the payments even with a $40,000 expansion which, because of inflation, bought much less than it had once purchased. However, they felt relatively secure because, although the value of the house wouldn't increase as much as the cost of the improvements, there was still a substantial amount of equity.

When the addition was completed, they would have $75,000 borrowed against a house that was probably worth $120,000; but they would enjoy it much more. The house should increase in value with inflation and the debt was not that bothersome. Suddenly, however, disinflation (or in some cases such as in Texas, deflation) occurred in the housing prices. In many cities, such as Houston, certain houses were either unsaleable for long periods or had to be reduced in price 30 percent or more. Now, these people in our example look at their neighbors having difficulty selling their houses and the lower prices they are receiving. They realize that their house might have to be liquidated in a deflationary environment at perhaps $80,000. And they have $75,000 still borrowed against it. Their debt has not changed since the house was worth $120,000, but their degree of leverage has changed dramatically. More importantly, they are concerned about being able to keep their jobs to maintain those house payments. As a result, they spend conservatively and have a slim margin for emergencies.

The factor of leverage is a very important one whether applied to an individual or an entire economy. Although it has always been a way to greatly enhance returns, it is a double-sided coin that can also cause accelerated and larger losses. Yet the reason that debt has been so popular in America has been the fluctuating inflation that we have had since World War II. We became accustomed to paying off debt in dollars worth less than the dollars we borrowed. Of equal importance is the fact that debt has been favored over equity by our tax structure. Interest is totally deductible while dividends are double taxed. So we have always had a propensity toward debt, but it has seldom been like we have seen in the last three to four years.

The increase in debt does not relate just to the deficits we have run with the national government. At some stage, Congress will be forced to address them. Of equal or greater consequence is the amount of debt that our American economic system has been undertaking privately and corporately. It is almost a direct result of the world international movement which led to deregulation of the financial system. It would be more appropriate to say the deregulation of *the financial or capital markets* than just the financial system itself which is often times thought to be banks and savings & loans only. The important distinction to remember regarding individual or government debt is that the amount is often less important than the value of the assets balanced against it and the cash flow the economy does or does not provide to gradually reduce it.

One of the most dramatic changes in the financial system occurred when banks were deregulated. In the 1960s, interest rates began rising, and pressure was placed upon the system. Money market funds emerged and attracted increasingly large deposits, as money left the regulated banks. In response, banks lobbied for looser regulations to allow them to pay varying interest on their deposits. Now banks enjoy limited regulation on the rates they can set for deposits.

This deregulation has also led to competition. In order to maintain deposits that the banks had already invested in loans or other investments or to increase their share of the market, they had to engage in intense competition for customers' money. Likewise, there has been a corresponding expansion of higher-rate loans or investments to offset increased costs. A banker is only a middle man. He rents one man's money to loan it to another. He must pay the person from whom he borrowed it, make a profit and pay his expenses from the money he receives from his borrower. That margin must also absorb any losses to credit quality.

Being a middleman is a difficult job today, not just in banking but in most fields. As the economy becomes much more efficient, it is squeezing out various levels. Airlines, communication, and a host of industries have seen it occur abruptly. We can observe this as discount stores move into smaller towns and replace five or six specialty stores that had carried a very limited inventory. Because of their large selection and discounted prices, the discount stores attract volumes of shoppers which keeps their costs down. That lets them make a smaller percentage on a much bigger sale volume and remain profitable, where many other stores are not able to exist at all. Now, there are not only discount stores, but super-discount stores in the form of clubs that give even further discounts. In effect, the middle men are removed from many portions of the economy. This has been happening in the financial systems as well.

For years, large commercial banks had a built-in market, since they were the source of funds for major corporations. But then securities dealers started placing major corporations' commercial paper on the market, where they could exchange large corporate notes between themselves at cheaper rates and avoid going through the banks. The savings and loan industry watched mortgage brokers and other groups enter their market areas. Entire financial systems have changed; the logic of the past doesn't necessarily fit the future. For many years, the savings & loans were encouraged to provide housing finance. In fact, that's why they were created and received tax and regulatory benefits. However, they generally would lend long on short-term funds. While the cost of their funds might go up within a year or less, their loans were usually made for 25 or 30 years. This created no problem, until inflation climbed in the late 1970s and interest rates followed. At one time, four and five percent mortgages had been good investments, but when money cost 12 percent to 13 percent, interest earnings on the loans became negative. Rural and branch banks had extensive amounts of money invested in bricks and mortar. They had been encouraged by the federal government to expand services. Then all of a sudden, competition, once minimal, now flooded banks in all forms ranging from credit cards to tremendous increases in the numbers of chartered banks.

Many states, such as California, gave new powers to savings & loans which allowed them to offer everything from real estate joint ventures to securities investments. With $100,000 per customer in federal insurance, they were able to expand on helpful leverage. Because the margin normally derived from lending had diminished, these new powers helped ease the burdens of the past years of low mortgage loans. But this also forced the industry into uncharted fields where it had little experience, and in many respects the banks followed. Banks, however, still lived under weightier restrictions than the savings & loans.

Competition within the financial marketplace escalated rapidly, and it changed far more than the public realizes. The significant rise and volatility in the stock market worried many people who thought that another stock market plunge similar to the one in 1929 would occur. Fortunately, the Federal Reserve's margin requirements have kept much better control of stock market speculation. Many people feel that the assets and earnings behind the various stocks have maintained the market's resiliency despite recent price fluctuation. My larger concern is the speculation taking place in the futures and options markets where, for relatively small amounts of money, you can bet on almost any occurrence. The markets are necessary for hedging, but trades are made far beyond the needs of our economy. That is the kind of speculative activity we should fear, as it is the subtle fringes which can unravel the larger fabric of the marketplace.

Speculation of this type is only one part of the problems emerging in the economy. We've seen a preponderance of new approaches such as leveraged buy-outs. In the leveraged buy-out, capital is removed from the market by the take-over of a company through issuance of large amounts of debt. As a result, there is less capital than there was before, and generous profits have probably been taken. The leverage provides tremendous returns for the limited amount of capital left, if the stock goes up in value and earnings are healthy. In that event, the debt usually can be paid by sale of assets. But if adverse economic conditions arise and asset sales are not feasible, or if the debt load becomes too large to be paid because of increased interest rates, that debt can take a company under very quickly. The leveraged buy-out, options, futures, and other creative financial instruments provide benefits by increasing market efficiency, if they are used for sound purposes. But they also contribute to a speculative binge for those willing to gamble. Corporate take-overs run risks also. While take-overs may enhance shareholder values through management restructuring, they often increase a company's debt.

All of this financial movement has reduced the amount of equity in the marketplace and mushroomed debt in proportions that have never occurred before. Paul Volcker, former Chairman of the Federal Reserve, has pointed out that the increased debt over the last several years is without historical precedent, except in highly disturbed economic circumstances such as depressions, wars, or major inflations. This debt build-up has disturbing implications for the economy. The Federal Reserve shows that indebtedness has grown at double-digit rates in each of the last three years; that is faster than our increases in income. Debt in the United States reached a total of $8.2 trillion in 1985, up from $4.3 trillion in 1979, which reflects huge federal budget deficits, business borrowing to finance highly leveraged mergers and acquisitions, and increased consumer borrowing to support spending habits.

The thing I fear as a banker is that debt has grown in a declining rate environment. If interest rates make exaggerated movements, it is questionable how well our economy will sustain its strength. The reason for this is the nature of the modern financial environment. The increasing volume and speed of transactions has become crucial. However, this tends to cut down the attention to credit worthiness. You must add to this the fact that juggling security for debt is precarious at best. Many institutions can now sell debt, such as home mortgages or various types of loans, to groups which package and resell them in the marketplace. Originating lenders care less about a borrower's long-term credit worthiness, if they know it will not be in their portfolio. Unfortunately, the purchaser thinks the security is like a bond in which he can trust. The paper looks the same; in reality, it is no better than the collateral behind it. Perhaps there is no better example than the Washington Public Power Supply System's default on several billion dollars of municipal bonds. People quickly purchased the bonds because they appeared secure, but the buyers had limited knowledge of the complicated transactions and fundamentals involved in the bonds or of how future unknowns could affect them. The same is true of a number of securities placed in today's markets that have to face the scrutiny and realities of a difficult economy.

Psychology is highly important in the financial markets. Risk is related to interest rate, and if investors' confidence is not maintained at optimistic levels, potentially greater problems lie ahead. The higher the interest rate required to maintain a line of credit or issue a replacement bond, the more pressure is placed upon a company because of its elevated debt leverage. Every percentage increase generates higher operating costs, and this most often occurs during difficult economic times which only adds to economic malaise. To complicate the situation, a large amount of foreign money flowed into our marketplace in the last three years. Now that our dollar is declining, which it needs to do to assist our trade balance, will foreign investors be willing to invest in America as they did in the past? If they don't, it's likely that the supply and demand factors of our financial system will drive up interest rates creating more pressure for leveraged companies. Currency exchange rates are a growing component in interest rate levels.

Our debt burden can be eliminated in a variety of ways. It can be achieved by gradual liquidation, although that solution seldom has been used in the past. That method requires dedication toward a goal with policies that have to be maintained through constant perseverance—just as a banker does when working out a longer payment period with a customer having trouble paying back a loan. While it's possible for government to enact those policies, it's unlikely that the politics of a democracy could coalesce sufficient support for such courage. Perhaps the best we can hope for is enough economic growth to reduce the amount of leverage within America. Then our income would cover existing debt payments, gradually reducing them over time. More importantly, we could reduce our degree of leverage by increasing our net worths with methods similar to our house buying example. This is the approach presently adopted by the international banks regarding their third world loans. The banks are attempting to keep loan levels relatively constant while assets and capital grow. Thus, they are in far better shape today than five years ago to absorb a default such as we feared by Mexico in the early 1980s. Actions by Citicorp and other banks to build a reserve for these loans show this is a method which can help address reality.

The other alternatives for reducing debt rapidly are not very positive. As we discussed, one way is through inflation. We did this in the

1970s and early 1980s. We repaid dollars with cheaper dollars and brought the economy into balance. It was a miserable experience which spawned economic recessions. Another way is through widespread default and liquidations of businesses. This is the process of bankruptcy in which losses are incurred by not paying debt. Liquidation builds a negative business environment which deters the optimism and expansion—two of the most important elements for a healthy economy. Texas has experienced more than its share of this type of adjustment in the 1980s and its unfavorable effect on people and our financial structure.

In summary, although regional economic conditions vary, we are faced with an existing debt overhang which is growing larger every year. We have international competition requiring us to make our companies leaner and stronger. We have a changing economy which has put some people out of work and searching for jobs. New areas of employment can be developed through research and innovative technology, but will require capital investment and increased economic growth in order to expand. Finally, our nation's psychological environment is critically important to the ultimate success of the economy. Over the last few years, income tax reductions and positive enhancements for business growth have been conducive to maintaining America's place in the world. But if our nation adopts a defeatist attitude like the one spreading in Europe, we will have almost insurmountable difficulty reaching our goals. Our national will to succeed is a requisite.

I have a friend, Clayton Williams, who is a successful oilman and rancher in Midland, Texas. He symbolizes one attitude found in Texas when he talks in private or appears on television shows such as "Nightline," where he said, "When a man loses what he's worked for during the past 25 or 30 years, it's going to break his heart in some way. But there is a resiliency here, and we are going to make it through this. We are caught in forces beyond our control. But if you have known men in combat, when they came through it, they had a closeness and a toughness that they didn't have before." Clayton has diversified by starting a telecommunications company as well as other businesses. The remaining natural resource is not oil and gas. It is, in effect, the natural resource of the people: our drive and determination to succeed.

In oil or any other industry, self-interest is one of the key ingredients of capitalism, and taxation greatly affects self-interest. The problem of finding the most effective level of taxation has haunted mankind for centuries. The issue is not as simple as people would have us believe. Taxes which occur at many levels and in many forms, have a cumulative effect.

Texas, for example, may have low state taxes but higher local taxes than another state.

The biggest single tax factor in economics, however, is the federal income tax because of its direct effect on the economy. According to Horace W. Busby and Associates, income was first taxed in 1914. The taxation rate was 1 percent. Single people received a flat $3000 exemption, and married couples had a $4000 exemption. Although 97 percent of the population did not even pay taxes, $41 million was raised that year from 3 percent of the population. World War I changed the tax picture. Congress increased the tax rate to 67 percent for individuals with an annual income over $2 million and later to 77 percent for individuals with incomes exceeding $1 million. Most people were enthusiastic about the tax, because very few of them had to pay it. Then, during World War II, people went into manufacturing and began earning higher wages. The income tax ceiling was lowered and many people had to pay taxes. Taxation met opposition, and its popularity began to decline. When first initiated, income tax raised only $47 billion between 1914 and 1943. With revenues needed for the war effort, the total tax collected between 1944 and 1963 amounted to $568.4 billion. Today's taxation yields that amount every 23 to 25 months. Despite this staggering figure, our nation is in debt, and the debt is growing.

There is substantial reason to question whether the income tax method of seeking revenues will be sufficient in the future to meet our country's needs. In all likelihood, we will be moving shortly to a new method of raising money in the form of consumption taxes. This would allow income tax rates to be maintained at present levels or reduced significantly. The massive amounts of money that have to be raised may be acquired through value-added-taxes or some nature of business transaction tax. Many people feel that a value-added tax would create an equitable tax structure, because the tax would be added to products as they moved through the manufacturing process. Therefore, whenever a product was purchased, the cost to the consumer would already include the tax. Manipulation of tax benefits, dodging sales taxes, or avoiding taxation through the underground economy would be eliminated. All strata of society would pay tax rather than placing the burden most heavily on the middle class. As more products were consumed, the tax revenue would increase. Tax dodgers would have to stop buying new television sets and other items which are viewed as necessities.

There are several ways to structure this form of taxation, and the prospects are bright that Congress may finally realize that the income tax system is not working effectively. The more a tax can be broadened over the entire economy that should be taxed, the smaller the burden on the individual taxpayer. Such a tax could be rebated by the government to make our exporters competitive, and most important of all, Congress will probably find it the only tax capable of raising the vast sums necessary if we continue on our present spending course. In view of the changing international situation, that would probably be a much more intelligent and competitive approach than our present system, particularly in light of the limited ability it will have to meet our future needs.

Horace Busby said in his publication, *The Busby Letters:*

". . . income tax is a failed system . . . and the fault of corporate taxation is known to every student of taxes: business does not pay taxes. Under the Constitution, private business cannot be prevented from passing along all taxes in its prices; the result, otherwise, would be confiscation.

So long as corporate income taxation remains, it serves as a refuge for politicians to give the public tax reductions with one hand while taking it back with the other."

Busby was a close adviser to Lyndon Johnson, yet he is respected by many of the Republicans because he is a superb analyst of positions, trends, and perspectives. His background and wisdom make this comment significant and worthy of careful attention.

Busby makes a unique observation in view of recent tax reform efforts in Congress—even more so considering the negative publicity given to President Reagan several years ago when he made a similar analysis. It's important for us to understand not only this point, but the total interrelationship of an intelligent, consistent strategy for our entire economic and political system. We can expect more benefit from a dedication to our common good, than we would lose from a diminished degree of self-interest. In fact, our self-interest often is even better served over time, when the common good is considered. Lincoln's words still remind us that united we stand, divided we fall.

The 1986 federal tax bill shifts taxes from individuals to business. It drops rates for both, but the true burden shifts. This will produce significant short-term economic pain and will not aid in capital formation which is necessary for long-term international competition. Eventually, we will need to address this problem, and the burden will be shifted again. But because of the negative aspects of raising personal tax rates and the enormous amount of money that must be raised, I feel we will see the value-added tax, securities tax, business transaction tax or similar concepts emerge. So tax reform is really only a beginning to a changed, but probably beneficial process—even though I feel it will have a much greater effect on the economy than is realized. In relation to the international business world, the lower tax rates for some types of businesses will even make us a tax haven and draw development.

As we look at many of the potential economic changes, we need to appreciate the importance of ideas. We are a nation of many opinions and concerns. Free enterprise has made us great. At the same time our moral fiber has been a key ingredient to our success and our ability to preserve democracy. Free enterprise and its modern equivalent of constructive capitalism have brought prosperity unequalled in the history of mankind to those who have followed its teachings.

We can control our economic and political destinies. If we create short-term solutions, accept hand-outs from the government and adopt policies that don't consider long-term effects, but only ease momentary pain, we inevitably will reap the consequences of our actions. On the other hand, if we are committed and know what economic and political policies we wish to pursue, we can move forward. The key to moving in a healthy direction lies within our character. As we have said before, character is destiny. Will we commit to educational programs which can build a foundation for technological awareness and the changes which will confront us; or will we be satisfied with mediocrity that condemns our children to a lower standard of living?

The question should not be: "Will America's standard of living decline?" but: "How much can it grow with the right policies?" There is a great difference between a 6 percent increase and a 3 percent increase in national growth, particularly over a period of time. One has only to look at the compound interest tables in the advertisements for Individual Retirement Accounts (IRAs) to realize the significance of this difference. The more growth, the more government can do without increasing taxes. Yet slower growth, or the absence of growth, and an increasing demand for services put a damper on business that keeps the cycle moving in the opposite direction.

The Texan "can do" spirit and determination to succeed has brought us out of difficult times in the past. There is little doubt that we have the right attitude to build a state of destiny, even in these times. But the question is whether attitude is enough. We still need a strategic and intelligent game plan. All of the effort in the world is useless, if we travel in circles. As Texans, we have to recognize our problems and find intelligent and consistent answers which will enable us to move forward in a positive direction. We must learn to be stewards of our state and national legacies of liberty and wealth. We need to recognize and promote statesmanship by forging long-term solutions rather than spewing rhetoric or promoting quick-fixes. If for every step forward we take two back, we can accomplish nothing.

"I know of no safe depository of the ultimate power of the society, but the people themselves."

—THOMAS JEFFERSON

IV.

RELATIONSHIPS OF IDEAS AND POLITICS WITHIN SOCIETY

Dad looked at life as a game of cards—in particular, a game of poker. He said that every card in the deck could be compared to a piece of information. You could arrange those cards, or pieces of information, in various ways—by color, suits, or sequence. In each case, the logic was simple to understand. However, in poker, as in life, all the cards are shuffled, dealt, and rearranged into logical groupings. The groupings might be straights, flushes, three of a kind, or jokers. What is crucial to a card game, and in life, is to understand not only where each card fits in the various groupings, but more importantly, what they mean when grouped together.

In the real world, the interrelationships between politics, economics, and the influence of the media can be as confusing as a poker game might be to someone who has never played. I realize now what Dad meant when he said that the difference between possessing information and possessing knowledge is the perspective a person applies to that information. Personal and civic judgment is refined by an understanding of history and *perspective* regarding the interrelationships of economics, politics, and communication. People cast their votes in the ballot box and in the market place with their dollars. Today, politics, business, and even the media often follow the people's inclinations rather than try to guide them.

89

As we exert our power to direct government, we need to understand how various segments of society interconnect in order to exercise our voice wisely. Basically, there is political power, economic power, and media power in our society. We need to understand each of these arenas, so that we can judge our leaders by their ideas. Understanding these relationships, we will be willing to sacrifice for a goal, because we believe in it personally. Sacrifice is only attained, however, when the majority of people are committed to a set of ideals.

As we pass through this time of transition and uncertainty, dissension is inevitable. We will be working out problems relating to the debt structure, international competition, funding difficulties, and social programs. Government doesn't create goods; it only redistributes them. So in order for government to give to someone, it has to take from someone else. Since this is the case, we must judiciously decide where scarce resources can be used for the best possible good and determine whether the public or private sectors should provide needed services. If we make the right choices, we will benefit in the long run.

Transition can be bewildering as we often are fighting enemies that we don't always understand, such as reduced social services, international competition, and economic difficulties related to debt problems. If it is any comfort, people have dealt with periods of change and uncertainty throughout history. In early times, disease caused uncertainty. When an epidemic or plague struck, the people panicked and seized any cure or blamed any convenient scapegoat for their troubles. More often than not, attempts at quick cures only hurt the body's natural resistance and gave the sick person a false hope of health. Modern science has replaced witch doctors and alchemists, and it has successfully cured many diseases. People today follow their doctor's advice because they have confidence in his expertise.

The critical point in the epidemic analogy is that we react strongly to perceived effects and benefits. Generally, we have confidence in medicine, while we are less certain about political mechanisms. I think the medical field gained our confidence because of the intelligent, painstaking and methodical way researchers worked on the challenge of disease control. First, they divided the problem areas, or diseases, into categories and then researched each in detail. They discovered symptoms, causes, and finally cures. Researchers were able to explain the relationship of the major causes of disease to hygiene and communication of germs. Then they developed cures such as pasteurization, vaccination, and other techniques. We were able to understand what they were doing, and we could judge the success of the remedies because they cured us or kept us healthy in the first place.

Despite these sophisticated cures, doctors affirm that a vital part of our recovery relates to mental outlook or confidence. I think the same is true in Texas as we feel the effects of the decline in oil prices, international trade competition, and the transition to an information society. If we are aware of structural changes taking place within our politics, economics, and media, our confidence in finding remedies to problems will increase tremendously. Awareness is the key.

Awareness is growing in many areas of Texas life. For example, our public educational system has failed to provide leadership and suffered a consequent loss of respect over the years. Yet, despite the problems of financing and debates over teaching methods and results, we now recognize the "disease," and we have begun to seek better quality instruction, academic excellence, and equity for all school districts. Even though we are not absolutely sure how we are going to achieve all our goals, our decision to value education as a way to assure high quality in life is correct. The direction of our trend is critical. If it is aimed in the proper direction, we need only concentrate on maintaining momentum.

Our awareness of problems in the criminal justice system also has increased. We've observed a system so favorable to criminals that some honest people began to turn their homes into high security prisons. If they walked out of the front door without turning off the alarm system, they had to immediately report themselves to their personal security network. From Dad's point of view, justice seemed to be lacking, even if the law was present. Fortunately, we are beginning to build more prisons, enhance criminal laws, and increase public awareness of crime. We are now recognizing the abuse of civil, malpractice, and product liability suits. Legal action against leaders serving on public and private boards has made many successful and able people afraid to participate because of concern for their families' security. It has gone so far that many competent people no longer seek office or provide leadership. I think we have become convinced that litigation has gone beyond reasonable limits, and reform is now underway with the compromise passed in the 1987 legislative session. A shift in emphasis will recognize individual rights by tempering our belief that "99 guilty people should go free to prevent one innocent person from being convicted" with the more modern concern of "what do 99 freed, guilty lawbreakers do to the rest of society?"

So through awareness of problems, our country's direction has begun to change, and both political parties at least have attempted to move toward more responsible government. However, we are seeing that global challenges loom in our future. We are addressing national crime, but terrorism is becoming a greater concern. Many of our solutions to education are based on adding more money to the system instead of dealing with the source of the problem—the basics of reading, writing, and arithmetic. However, the money flow is beginning to be cut back in an attempt to reduce our national deficit. As that happens, Texans will be faced with those same difficult choices. Higher taxes can affect our economic growth and reduce incentives for businesses to locate here as well as burden our people. Decline in education hurts growth. Thus, our decision-making has to be balanced, thoughtful, and visionary so that our actions benefit each interconnected area of life.

We still see major problems with the infrastructure we have built over many years. Our highways, city services such as water and sewage treatment and other areas essential to commerce need additional revenue for maintenance, but money is short for these needs also. The arts and cultural elements of society, which enrich our quality of life and add depth and understanding to our existence, have already experienced reduction in funding. Jobs are being lost to the workers in other countries. Some feel rich citizens are getting richer, while our poor are growing poorer. That trend hurts any democracy, where justice depends on a large and strong middle class.

So even though we're changing and moving into the unknown, we've got to recognize and plan for these and other emerging problems. In fact, there are so many different areas that need attention, we have to decide which to attack first. Just looking at the sores and trying to predict where another one might erupt can sometimes divert our attention from curing the actual disease. If we recognize that these potential problems are the symptoms of a much larger weakness in our society, we have made progress toward the solution.

At present, that weakness is largely caused by indecision in our collective will. We are loathe to take decisive actions which will position us for the future. We speak of our trade deficit as resulting from our federal deficit. But the budget deficit is caused by our inability in the political arena to decide the role of government on other than individualized political issues. Using the methodology of medical research, we must first find the ways a particular disease spreads, gain people's confidence by showing that our approach and direction are sound, and only then begin to apply cures.

Perhaps the most critical disease, and one which encompasses all of the others, is pressure to maintain our average standard of living. A strong economy and high standard of living lead to better education, greater opportunities and a positive psychological viewpoint, thus creating a desire to get the best out of life and society. Quality of life is often well-defined by whether one has a job and how good the job is, since that is a major factor determining a person's ability to have the time and resources to enjoy life.

If we come together and work for the common good, thereby increasing our own standard of living, we will have a chance to solve our problems. However, if we decide to fight over the spoils and divide into special interests, I believe Texas and the rest of the United States will begin an irreversible decline. It's not just a question of economics. It's a question of government and our perception of ourselves and where we are headed. These issues are reflected and defined through the media. Our political system determines our economic system by its taxation policies, regulations, and general structure. It plays an important role in international trade through the adoption of policies that promote fair trade rather than protectionism. The media's contribution is to help us understand the real causes of problems and the solutions available to us. Another function of the media is to explain perceptions which often cloud the real issues and their alternatives. The media can provide a vital service by offering a clear and accurate appraisal of situations and a well-rounded analysis of all sides of economic and political issues.

History can help us ferret out the importance of adjusting the structures under which we live. As in Dad's analogy about the creek, if you came upon a stream two days in succession, things were the same, yet they were different also; and it was important to see those differences. The scene was the same. The bank, trees, and the setting had not changed noticeably. But the water that had been there the day before was now long past. Dad, who was a student of history, emphasized that certain values existed in all successful societies. They were time-tested. They benefited people and kept society strong and vital, which is why people tried to protect them. At the same time he said we should learn about trends from history to give us insight into today's transitions and directions.

He also used what I call the pot roast story to make his points. The story is about a granddaughter who prepared a roast for her husband. Each time she cooked this meal, she bought a very special piece of meat, cut off and put aside about 1/4 of the end and cooked the rest. One evening, her husband asked her why she did that, and she replied that her mother had always done it that way. Later, realizing she'd never known the reason, she asked her mother why she always cut off a portion of the roast. Her mother said that she had learned to prepare a roast in that manner from her mother, and she was sure that there was an important reason for it, since her mother was an excellent cook. When the family had a reunion, both daughter and granddaughter asked the grandmother why she cut 1/4 off the end of a roast before cooking it. She answered very logically that she cut off the end piece of her roasts because she had a very small roasting pan. We need to understand the reason for any action we take to be sure we are proceeding in a logical direction.

The challenges we face today are not new. We can learn much about cures and solutions for these problems from the experiences of others. A decade has passed since the United States' bicentennial celebration, and it appears the path to the third-hundred-year milestone will provide our greatest tests as well as our greatest moment. When our nation was in its infancy, Patrick Henry said, "I have but one lamp by which my feet are guided, and that is the lamp of experience. I know of no way of judging the future but by the past." Our founding fathers wrote the Constitution and Declaration of Independence during a time of mental and spiritual enlightenment. Many of the fundamental principles underpinning our nation and form of government were inspired by an understanding of morality and the importance of preserving individual choice and individual rights.

At that time, Edward Gibbon was writing his *Decline and Fall of the Roman Empire* which highlighted the importance of individual responsibility. Adam Smith broadened awareness of the free enterprise system in his *Wealth of Nations*. When America's fundamental documents were written, our forefathers realized that other forms of democracy had eroded with time. The Greek Empire was perhaps best described by a comment attributed as far back as Socrates: "When the masses of the people find that they can vote themselves prosperity from the public treasury, a democracy is no longer possible." That happened in Athens during Socrates' lifetime. And it's an observation repeated by many leaders of other societies from that time forward.

The Roman Empire can teach us a great deal, since many of its characteristics can be seen in western civilization today. Kitty's uncle, the late Steele Wright of Nacogdoches, Texas, once gave me an article that included a summary of observations about Gibbons' book. Though I have never been able to find the source material, the article listed five basic reasons why Rome withered and died. The reasons given were: "(1) the sanctity and dignity of the home were undermined; (2) taxation became higher and higher, with public money being spent for free bread and circuses for the people; (3) there was a mad craze for pleasure and violence, and sports became more exciting, brutal and immoral as people grew increasingly desensitized; (4) armaments were built when the real enemy was the decay of individual responsibility; (5) religion degenerated into mere form and lost its touch with life and no longer had the power to guide people in spiritual directions." Other historians have disagreed with Gibbon's analysis. They contend that he had the right facts, but the wrong conclusions. To them, the protracted economic decline was the cause of the fall. The crucial point is that both morality and economics are key to the strength of a society, and they bear a relationship to each other.

For some reason, I had always thought that the more people discovered and learned, the more their accomplishments and quality of life improved. But when I studied a graph depicting the Meso-American civilizations of the Toltecs, the Aztecs, Incas, and the Mayans in the Museum of Anthropology in Mexico City, I was stunned. These societies rose and fell just like Greece and Rome. The graph took each civilization and plotted it in a time frame in relation to how many tools and household implements it had at different periods of history. Each society had progressed in a type of bell curve. It reached a high point in the number of implements it had, and then these numbers decreased as the society gradually faded and was finally destroyed. In some cases, societies were invaded, such as the Aztecs by Cortez and the Spaniards. But regardless of what caused the final collapse, often the internal society within each civilization usually deteriorated first.

As you study the decline of these and other states and nations, you see that a pattern emerges. A type of what I will call disease strikes each group of people after they reach a high point in their quality of life. The principal symptom appears to be an erosion of individual responsibility. This progressively weakens the society and its people and the work ethic in which each person earns his own way.

When a state or republic is first formed, people are drawn together for a common purpose. Most of the time the motivation is economic. On occasion, it is religious. Everybody's standard of living improves through joint commerce. Together they build an ever-increasing pie. The bigger the pie gets, the more there is for all. But as civilization progresses, the emphasis shifts from increasing the pie to dividing it. At that point, people split into groups, and each group's primary concern is getting the biggest piece possible for its members, thus expanding laterally, instead of increasing the size of the pie for everyone. Once this shift takes place, the nature of our society changes too. We look out for "Number One" and grab everything we can for ourselves through the courts, business, and even our social and religious lives. Our preoccupation with self-gratification slowly and deliberately pervades society, and our once-strong values of simplicity, honor, courage, morality, and ethics are neglected and even laughed at as being old-fashioned and out of place in the modern world of pragmatism.

This forsaking of individual responsibility is, in my opinion, the real root of the evil or disease plaguing us. We no longer feel we have to vote or take any action or work to stop crime. We expect to be led and cared for and government is pressured to do so. We criticize our leaders and often choose them unwisely based on flimsy promises. Only we, the people, can mold our national destiny. Our leaders can't do it for us. They need our support in order to be statesmen. Otherwise we will continue to elect weak politicians whose only goal is to please special interest groups and maybe get mentioned in a history book. We can follow a good leader, but it is our strength as individuals and our willingness to sacrifice for a greater reward in the future that make change possible. Unfortunately, in our present mood, asking us to sacrifice often is like asking us to drink poison. A call for sacrifice is the fastest way to kill anybody's political career. So not only have we abandoned our individual responsibility, but we have restricted our leaders in the amount of good they can do for us. John Stuart Mill expressed it this way: "A state which dwarfs its men, in order that they may be more docile instruments in its hands, even for beneficial purposes, will find that with small men, no great thing can really be accomplished."

Texans are unique. Individual responsibility and a willingness to co-operate are still part of our character and give muscle to our society. In the past America has had two coasts of thought—the east and west. I believe that what we need now is emergence of another viewpoint. Our Texas values can contribute much to a national destiny. We can be a third coast of thought. Our country is now drifting, without many of its old guiding principles, as it searches for solutions among various alter-natives. But there are no quick solutions, and our greatest achievements will come as a result of perseverance instead of brute force.

My first real experience in politics took place outside of the Brenham courthouse during a period of transition and turmoil in Texas. Dad was in the Sheriff's office on the second floor. I was playing with some other kids on the courthouse lawn waiting to ride home with him. Suddenly I saw a huge shadow fall on the grass. I looked up. A man was staring at the Shivercrat button which one of Dad's friends had given me. I was using it as a sheriff's badge. He snarled something about me being that Dippel kid whose father was supporting Shivers and said he planned to vote Dad out of office for backing Shivers. Then he told me to give Dad that message. I raced up the two flights of stairs to Dad's office, afraid that by wearing the button I had done something which would cause Dad to lose his job, and we would all starve.

Dad wasn't concerned about his job, but he was irritated that a grown man would try to intimidate kids. He obviously saw that I was very confused, and we had one of our earliest discussions about the realities of life. We talked about the differences between conscience and convenience in life and particularly in politics. He had friends who were leaders of both factors of the Democratic Party at that time, and there was a lot of pressure on him, because he had considerable political influence and each side needed his help.

Dad explained that the Democratic Party had been critically important in Texas since the Reconstruction years following the Civil War. Republicans had been considered very dictatorial during Reconstruction, and as a result conservative Democrats had united to regain control of the government after Reconstruction ended. A staunch Democratic base was established at that time. That power base was broadened during the Depression in the 1930s. As a consequence of this tremendous public support for the Democratic Party, there had been no Republican presence of significance in the state, and almost all local officials were elected as Democrats.

But now a conflict had arisen that pulled at the soul of each voter in the state. Education was the only thing that could help Texas expand from its agricultural base to a diversified economy, and that took money. The climax came one hot August afternoon in 1952, when Governor Shivers drew a political line in Springfield, Illinois which changed the course of Texas politics.

On that day he told Illinois Governor Adlai E. Stevenson that he was going to support Republican Dwight D. Eisenhower for President of the United States. Governor Stevenson was horrified since he was the newly-nominated Democratic candidate for president. He knew that without Texas' support, he'd have a hard time winning a presidential election. Shiver's step was bold, and many of his Democratic colleagues were enraged. But to Governor Shivers, the issue rested on the principle of states rights and the revenue which Texas needed for its schools. Both Presidents Roosevelt and Truman had thwarted Texas' interests by claiming that royalties from offshore territory, called the Tidelands, should go to the federal government instead of the state. Shivers knew that the land had been given to Texas when it became part of the United States in 1846. It had been set aside as a commitment to education and our future. Dwight Eisenhower agreed to support Texas' claim to the proceeds from that land, and the battle lines between party and principle were drawn.

The race between Eisenhower and Adlai Stevenson was a difficult choice between good men on both sides. Was party loyalty most important or were the issues? There was no question that whichever side a man took, he would face opposition. The important thing was to be right. During our discussion, Dad told me that *leaders could be classified by whether their primary motivation was conscience or convenience.* There were men who did what they felt was right and those who did what they felt was popular. Dad supported Shivers wholeheartedly because he said our political choices had to be prioritized. In his mind, personal loyalty belonged first to God, then your country, and finally to your political party. If your party's actions were in conflict with the other two priorities, then you needed to work within the party to change it. If you didn't, you had a problem of conscience. Party loyalty was very important to him, but he believed the reason for a party's existence was to offer and provide the best in government.

However, those who enforced party loyalty through fear and coercion were offensive to Dad. He said that Hitler's book, *Mein Kampf,* stated correctly that the most effective way to destroy ideas was through intimidation and force, and you needed to be skeptical of anyone using those tactics whether you agreed with them or not.

Dad told me not to worry, to wear the button, and if the man said anything else to tell him that dad was upstairs and would be happy to talk with him. I went back down, and at the time I thought I understood most of what had been said. Later, I realized how serious that conversation was. Watching Governor Shivers stand on principle while keeping the respect of other people proved to me that doing what's right pays off, but not without costs. Sam Rayburn, the Speaker of the U.S. House of Representatives, probably lost his chance at the presidency because of that party split, and the resultant party battles between Shivers and the LBJ/ Rayburn factions seriously divided the state.

It has always amazed me how insignificant the roots of major events can appear. Many historians believe that World War II really began when Japan shelled some mud huts in Manchuria, and no one opposed them— years before Germany's initial assaults. Yet from those seemingly inconsequential attacks, a global war followed. A parallel could be drawn to what was happening in Texas. What first appeared to be a small political event touched off a transition period in our history. Texans have always been independent thinkers, and as we have become better-educated, we have developed into a much more thoughtful society. The elections of John Tower and Bill Clements can be traced to this independence of thought. Now both the Republican and Democratic parties have to realize that Texans no longer vote solely out of party loyalty in either direction. We expect the party to provide ideas and a philosophy of government as an umbrella under which candidates can run. We also expect the party to offer more in the sense of solutions and principles, for the future will be significantly different from the past, and our political structure is the one way that government can be affected by the people's will.

I think more people gave elected officials the benefit of the doubt on political and policy decisions during the 1950s than do today. This trust developed because voters often knew their state candidates. When people know and trust someone, they usually support them through the tough times. That is still true today. In the 1980s, however, it's difficult to get to know individual candidates, and if we try to vote for what's right by just sticking to a party label without considering whether the party's ideas are sound, then we risk supporting ideas which could go against our personal conscience and ethical code.

Shiver's decision to support Texas over his party's interests did more than just anger Democrats. It made people look to ideas, rather than labels, and opened the door for other political parties to grow in our state. It took a long time, but now you meet Texans who endorse Republican, Independent, Libertarian, and other political philosophies. As the saying goes, "Before, people just bought the bottle because it was pretty and never read the label." Today people are more discriminating in their choice of candidates. It is not so much party realignment as a dealignment for parties with individualism becoming a controlling force. This also explains in part the difficulties office holders face in accomplishing particular goals. In the past, parties were more clearly defined and usually controlled both the executive and legislative branches when a party was "in power." This made it easier to promote legislation for specific ends. Today, the attention centers on individual candidates instead of the political party, making it harder to reach consensus on goals. The influence of regionalism in Washington politics adds an additional burden to accomplishing goals.

Texans have always held their public servants accountable. We expect limited government when there is no crisis. But we also expect government to act when trends change and things need to be done. Voters want to see actual accomplishment instead of mere rhetoric. However, given society's present level of understanding and unwillingness to sacrifice for a goal, no politician or statesman can alter our course. Good leaders in office certainly help; and they are a necessity, but without the backing of the people, their reforms will be diluted by the legislature, the executive office, the courts, and our silent but powerful bureaucracy. As

Ronald Reagan noted, "Government controls the economy, and bureaucracy controls government and has since the days of Franklin Roosevelt." The Reagan revolution tried to initiate massive changes by throwing out many programs rather than changing them gradually. Gradual changes within a democracy inevitably lose momentum and have little impact. If we want to make major changes, we must affect all parts of the government—including the courts and the bureaucracy—and make each branch more responsive to the people.

Potentially, we have the power to make these changes by working within acceptable channels. There is much power available to us as long as the mood of the people supports a directional shift. We need to elect people who are guided by their hearts as well as their intellects. As the Roman emperor, Marcus Aurelius, noted, "A man should be upright, not be kept upright."

I see our greatest strength and potential for positive change and solutions resting in our middle class. Texas was built by a middle class of men and women who, like ourselves, believed in making their own way and supporting their families. In general, we are a moral people who believe in personal freedom. We have taken advantage of this country's opportunities for unlimited advancement through work. We have always been our greatest asset.

Of all the problems facing Texas and the rest of the United States, history shows that we should deal first with our economic problems. In the modern world, economics is not independent from government. In 1928, government spending was about 10 percent of our gross national product. Today it accounts for well over one-third of our GNP. The most difficult choice we face in this transition period is which method to use in organizing our economic activity. Budget deficits will force us to decide between spending cuts and increasing reliance on the private sector to perform services previously provided by government, or we can raise taxes and maintain or enhance existing programs. We must choose wisely. If we do not define our direction clearly, we risk the problem of gridlock. It's like the man who had a headache. One doctor told him to apply a hot water bottle to his throbbing temples. Another said to use an ice pack. Since he wanted quick relief, the man thought he'd take the best of both cures, so he mixed the hot and cold water together and placed that combination on his head. Of course the remedies had no effect on his headache, and he concluded that both doctors were wrong. We have to understand the logic of our actions.

Basically, there are only two ways to organize our economic activity. We can solicit voluntary cooperation or use coercion—freedom or force.

I believe that all societies are mixtures of these two approaches. Over time, Americans have drifted away from a free market, consumer-choice economy and toward a centrally-planned society. Now we are contemplating a return to the former. We have used problems to justify increasing government power to manage and control the economy and our personal lives. When Reagan took office, we saw some movement away from central control. We spoke of deregulating society, reducing taxation, and limiting the role of government. But, in effect, we have only slowed government's growth. As President Reagan's term ends, the question will emerge: which method should be used to solve our problems. Because of his personal popularity, and our trust in him, Reagan has had an opportunity to lead us through his personal magnetism rather than by our understanding of his exact policies. Many of these policies have not been formulated with much detail or economic theory. Instead, the country has simply moved in a general direction.

When Reagan is no longer at the helm, the Republican and Democratic parties will face difficult choices. They'll have to address the method by which they intend to solve our economic dilemmas. We hear lots of terms thrown around by politicians and the media—from strategic planning to free market economics to industrial planning. But the people, as a whole, have already spoken. *And the message is that we want a reduction in government.* That is not to say that we don't want the government to help the needy; it is just that government is inefficient in getting funds and services to people. Government agencies are not responsive to the pressures of profit and loss. Yet their decisions can affect management results, while they have no management responsibilities. This creates an unresponsive economy in a time when we need to adapt to aggressive competition from outside our borders.

Generally, people don't recognize that our economy and government are so interconnected, and the media is the lens which filters the information we receive about both. We do know, however, that we are in difficult times, and we should be serious about getting the economy in order. We become uneasy about anything that seems to hinder that goal. If we understand this close relationship between economy and government and know that regulatory and taxing power affect our direction, it becomes crucial that we look at one of the fundamentals Ronald Reagan pointed out in his book, *Call to Action:*

"Continued government growth was an invention of Franklin Roosevelt's New Deal. Roosevelt's Secretary of the Treasury, Henry Morgenthau, Jr., gave it impetus by deciding to use taxing power for regulation of behavior. He even said publicly that taxes were intended to both punish and reward behavior that the government wanted to discourage or encourage. Since then it has been incorrect to think of taxes only as the most efficient means of raising money needed by government. They have become an economic and social tool of government social reformers to control our actions and choices."

It is important to understand how critical tax reform has become in influencing the direction of our economy. We're not merely talking about increasing the amount of take-home pay. If we steer to the wrong port, our standard of living will be significantly lower. Efficient steering will require some degree of sacrifice during the transition from special interests toward the common good. However, we must also follow the fundamental laws of economics, because we will inevitably face the consequences of breaking them. It is a fallacy that government can make laws without regard to those principles. If a man jumps off a cliff, he does not break the law of gravity, it breaks him. He may delay his fall by grabbing onto trees growing out of the cliff, but he will continue the downward plunge. We are like that man. If we use a parachute, we descend slowy, enjoying the ride and excitement. But we forget we are going down until we reach the bottom and have to think about how to climb back up. It is very encouraging that the final tax bill passed in 1986 embraced the Senate's 15 percent/ 28 percent tax compromise. This Senate version, which was finally passed by Congress rather than the original House version, acknowledged the need for fundamental, strategic reform. I predict we will refine our policies even further, particularly when the burden on business is understood. But finally, we are endorsing an economy driven by economic motivations, not tax benefits, and that is very positive for our competitive position.

But where do trends in other areas lead? When making our choices, we need to recognize that all parts of society—economics, politics, and our culture upon which society rests—are completely interrelated. Right now many educated and knowledgeable people are telling us what we should worry about and where we should assign priority. It reminds me of a story about a scientist who decided to study the reflex actions of a flea. He found a healthy six-legged specimen. After much effort, he succeeded in getting the flea to hop over his thumb at the command, "Jump." The scientist decided to experiment. He snipped off two of the flea's legs, shouted "Jump," and the flea still hurdled his thumb. Then he removed two more legs. The flea, tottering now, still managed to get over the thumb. The scientist then snipped off the last two legs and shouted

"Jump." But the flea didn't move. The scientist went to his desk and wrote his findings as follows: "When you remove all the legs of a flea, it becomes deaf." There are many ways to read history and economics, and we need to be careful that our observations are logical and our advisors free of self-interest.

We can make observations about society, but going back to our roots, to our particular, personal experience, gives each of us a broadened perspective. In the final analysis, one's own experience and reading will be the litmus test for his view of the world. As I think back on those early years in Brenham and the advice Dad gave me, I recognize that the values and ideas I learned were no different from what other people have learned. By studying history, I realized that much of the western world's wisdom had not been gained by finding the *quick solutions*. Instead, it began by asking the *right questions,* which ultimately produced new discoveries and concepts and changed the direction of whole societies. The Texas of my youth valued entrepreneurship, the work ethic, and an appreciation for opportunity. Today we still hold firmly to these roots, and we also understand the need for a technological and international future.

We are looking for new ideas. More of us are better educated than ever before, and thanks to the media, we've seen more world events and grappled with greater ethical questions than most of our ancestors. The more we are pressed by difficulty, the more intense our attention must become. For the first time since World War II, we are realizing how much is really at stake and how difficult times can get. While short-term, good economic news may ease the nation's immediate concerns, thinking people know that problems still exist. It is time to mobilize, and never in our nation's history has there been such a pressing need to sound the call for individual responsibility.

You might be one of those people today who don't have a party affiliation. Your decisions on candidates are based on a set of ideas, principles, or perhaps particular issues. Individuals not affiliated with a party are often called the swing voters. They are hard to classify and only amount to a small but steadily growing percentage of the electorate. However, this group is nearly always the deciding factor in elections and will be increasingly so in the future. They usually favor a particular issue or point of view and then vote according to which candidate most closely agrees with that viewpoint. The outcome becomes very difficult to predict because these people can easily swing an election, and you don't often know how they will react.

Other people today say that they don't vote any more because politics is just a matter of buying a candidate, and they don't have any hope of affecting the political process. In their perspective, candidates pay more attention to people who have money. Special interest groups raise funds for financing campaigns in hopes that they can gain the winner's ear after election day. That tactic can backfire, since some politicians use their opponent's contribution lists for punishing individuals and companies which did not support them. Giving money is a two-edged sword. It helps you gain access to a politician, but it can be used against you. Consequently, many people and groups give to both sides with slightly more going to the one they wish to win. But that is counterproductive if you have a clear preference since money's value diminishes once certain levels are reached in a campaign.

Then there are people who can afford to contribute money to political campaigns, but do not because they have an ethical problem with the way our election system operates. Others just don't understand how the system really works, and that lack of understanding makes them ineffectual. Lack of understanding, money, or a strong sense of idealism often combine to make people helpless in the face of a complicated political structure where ethics are rarely practiced.

In times past, Texans who lived in rural areas felt in control of our political destiny because our close connections to a party gave us a sense of belonging to a group. We knew each other which created trust and loyalty among us. Information was filtered through the party pipeline, so we knew more about what was happening politically even though that news was colored by the party's perspective. It is significant that in Governor Bill Clements' 1986 victory, the rural areas, for the first time in a state election, truly broke from a strong Democratic tradition. It marked a new day in Texas politics.

However, we now have more access to information on world and national events through the media, which has encouraged an ever greater independence of thinking. The Vietnam War and Watergate showed that our leadership was not infallible. Misjudgements and miscalculations occurred. Some of us thought that a full scale war should have been waged while others believed that the U.S. should have never gotten involved. Some national leaders believed that the public should not be privy to decisions made in Washington, such as the time Nixon's administration decided to move troops into Cambodia without fully informing Congress. After Nixon resigned, we overreacted by pulling in our muscle abroad. Pride in our national leadership weakened, and other nations accused us of impotence.

People who supported a party or an administration without question discovered that blind allegiance did not necessarily mean they were more patriotic than people who questioned political decisions. As a result, I think that some Americans became very discouraged for a number of years. Many young people dismissed politics altogether, which led to a growing feeling of helplessness when it came to exercising a voice in government. Their view of government, shaped by the idealism of the Kennedy era, had ignited civic interest and patriotic pride.

This new lack of interest in politics was fodder for sociologists, psychologists, and political scientists. Some said the "Me" generation was only interested in momentary pleasures. The process of learning about politics and issues took too much time and effort—it wasn't immediately gratifying. Others said that our upward mobility and loss of the extended family and community contributed to a feeling of alienation and powerlessness. Psychological support and peer pressure to contribute to our communities diminished. We became isolated in brand-new suburbs or glittering cities.

In the 1960s, we were accused of performing rituals without meaning or thought, following roles which enslaved our hearts and minds, behaving as faceless beings in a sea of faceless humanity. Our artists pointed to the problems of society, and groups formed to bring togetherness and quality to life through new communities and social networks. Some adults reverted to child-like egocentricity. Others were fooled into a false security believing that if they surrounded themselves with pleasures and self-indulgence, the world would be safe and secure. This only further alienated them from exercising real personal power. Some experts said that the world was becoming smaller. We saw all the world's problems every evening in color on a small screen, and many of us began to feel overwhelmed and helpless to control the forces at work.

After the sense of political betrayal, anger, and apathy subsided, we were ready to take self-government more seriously. We had learned a lot. The media served as our private political investigator and teacher. Through the eyes of reporters and journalists, we learned the hard lesson that politics had always been a lot dirtier and less ethical than our civics teacher told us. It was like a building going through an earthquake. The entire structure was pushed and pulled in every direction. The foundation heaved, and some of the windows fell out. Its occupants were shaken but unharmed. Importantly, we were realizing what tremendous power government had in our lives and how much its actions affected us personally—such as its ability to affect inflation. For reasons of self-interest, we had to be involved in the system.

When Ronald Reagan ran for president, many voters were ready. Reagan's political strategy was sound. He stood for ideas we perceived as good. Americans had a strong government and more freedom than most nations. We were not hopeless nor powerless. We wanted to know more about how politics worked, and how we could be part of the process. We realized that we had the power to set the country back on an even keel. Reagan symbolized that power and vitality, and we elected him.

If we talk about "power in politics," others may assume that we intend to use that power against them. This is understandable, because power too often has been used to benefit some people at the expense of others. Yet I believe that personal and political power is a healthy quality. When we use it to improve our own lives at no one else's expense, power becomes an exercise of personal freedom. It can also be used to serve other people.

Frequently, people resent anyone who tries to be a leader, but we need to realize that some type of leadership must and will occur. The question, then, becomes whether a leader's direction is helping or harming us. Generally, active leadership is positive, because it shows reaction to a problem. There is an old saying that if you put a frog in a pan of water and turn up the heat, he can jump or he can boil. It is his choice. Similarly, leadership comes in reaction to problems. If that leadership has merit, it should be commended and supported. Edmund Burke pointed out that "all that is necessary for evil to prevail is for good men to do nothing."

In like manner, we need power in our lives in order to create the best possible environment for our personal growth. Some people are content to live without questioning what the government bureaucrats do or how politicians run our state and nation. And there are those who crave absolute power over the lives of others. Most of us, however, are somewhere between these two extremes. We have been taught that as citizens of Texas and the United States we are expected to participate in government. Yet we have seen power and control slip out of our hands. Society has become more mobile. Solid political networks weaken as we move away from our hometown nucleus of information and support. We find homes in large cities, brand new suburbs, or established communities. Regardless of the location, getting settled in new jobs and adapting to different customs takes a lot of time. We often don't become acclimated to the political network for a number of years, unless our employment helps that transition by putting us in touch with the political structure.

So we're faced with living in a new town, maybe a new state, and we are trying to adjust. At the same time we want more power in our economic and political lives. When I returned to Brenham, I had to prove myself. I had to build my own network, although Dad's friends helped a great deal. Whether you come of age in Texas or move here from out-of-state, most people eventually start exercising some degree of leadership. Whether you're at a school board meeting, distributing yard signs for a favorite candidate, lobbying your state representative, or listening to candidates on television, the process can be confusing. That's because there are so many different worlds of politics. Each has its own distinct rules. To understand political power, as separate from economic or media power, we need to realize that it is a more personal medium. Economics and media are directed toward the general population. Politics shares the same characteristics, but the individual leaders are human, and their idiosyncrasies and interests do as much to define the political landscape as the general ideas of the media and economics.

Political leaders often draw a parallel between war and politics. You might be successful at some skirmishes, but the important goal is to win the war. Likewise, while it's important to elect a wise governor or congressman, it's far more important to influence a government. If the government can be influenced to adopt basic changes, incentives, and ideas that uplift people's lives, then we can make some solid and long-lasting contributions through politics. Our success could have powerful effects, as did the great Reformation in 16th century Europe. The question is, how can we understand and influence government today?

To begin, the world of "politics" is multifaceted. In electoral politics, your goal is to elect a president, governor, senator, representative and other government officials. There's excitement in campaigning, developing strategy, competing against another political team, and fighting to get your goals and beliefs into government. It's hard work, but you're teamed up with like-minded people which gives a feeling of camaraderie. Texas elections feature glittering parties in Dallas and Houston and outdoor barbeques in Amarillo and Tyler. Organization and lots of money become crucial to success in electoral politics.

Legislative politics start after the election. This involves writing, debating, and passing bills, funding agency budgets, and allocating taxpayers' money. Power is not necessarily equal under legislative politics as it is under electoral. Each politician represents a certain number of people. Therefore, it's natural to assume that each representative's voice is equal in the House or Senate. That is a wrong assumption, which can be extremely frustrating to a newly-elected official or to a citizen-lobbyist who might be in Austin for the first time with good ideas but little background in legislative politics. Effective power belongs to chairmen of key committees such as appropriations, ways and means, calendar rules, or specific committees having special jurisdiction. Those chairmen may have more power in determining the success or failure of a particular issue in legislative politics than all of the other legislative members combined. If that issue does not emerge from one of these committees, for all intents and purposes it is dead. The Speaker of the House and the Lieutenant Governor have significant power because they appoint the committees.

So while we have direct input into who is elected, power quickly shifts away from the voters when elected officials get to Austin or Washington. We may have voted for someone because we liked his stand on a fiscal issue. Yet once that person sits on the floor of the House or Senate, he is required to decide on thousands of issues other than the one we were interested in. This is where the power starts to flow. This is where we need to know that our representatives are statesmen who will look after our local interests while making sure that other people are not hurt at the same time.

The third form of politics is the bureaucracy which includes government agencies. In many ways, the three political worlds are similar, but each requires a different strategy. If we want to instill a set of ideas in government, we have to understand all three worlds. No matter who is elected governor or president, the nature of our system can be frustrating, since the checks and balances act as safety valves for ideas which benefit limited interests. At the same time, ideas that serve the greatest good for all concerned often get lost among the counterbalances.

You might elect a governor who promises to pass a bill favoring industrial development. The governor can make appointments to an industrial development board, but if the legislature does not give that board the money to operate, it cannot be effective. Each political world is unique and fascinating, because of the different skills required. Even if you never become politically active beyond voting, this knowledge is important for making informed decisions on candidates and policy.

However, we have the ability to affect our politicians more now than voters were able to do in the past. Years ago, ideas were discussed in greater depth. There was more time for deliberation and thought. Today, emotion prevails. If a politician wishes to stay in office for his own ego or career, or a statesman wants to be around long enough to make a change for principle, both must understand the reality of the modern political system. The volatility of the voters in recent elections has been pronounced. We have been looking for leadership and direction, but we've been concentrating on short-term, single issues. Because of that short-term view, almost everyone in electoral or legislative politics positions himself very carefully, according to what he thinks the people want, as indicated by opinion polls. Therefore, the individual is important. To understand how important, it is necessary to have a realistic picture of how a campaign actually operates.

Campaigning is the phase of electoral politics where candidates make promises and concentrate on finishing ahead of their rivals. If you work in a campaign or want to influence the outcome, you'll have to operate within certain rules of the game. Political parties still provide the machinery that gets your candidate elected, although the ideas you find within political parties today don't always agree with the party's stated position.

When we think about politics, perhaps the first scenes which come to mind are the media events: a candidate speaking or shaking hands and thousands of people cheering. This gives the impression of absolute organization, brilliant salesmanship, and careful packaging by highly paid professional advisors. It is a rare campaign that has even a few of these ingredients. If you watch a variety of races in politics over a long period, you find that the circumstances of timing and luck often have as much to do with political success as brilliant electioneering. Depending on the importance and nature of the race, name identification alone is important. The mere fact that a candidate's name has a certain sound or appears first on the ballot can do as much good as major advertising. Many worthwhile candidates have lost elections simply because their less competent opponents had better name recognition. When no name is recognizable, the party becomes a consideration, particularly in elections such as city judgeships.

In higher-profile races where an indication of conservative or liberal leanings can be inferred, the public generally demonstrates only limited degree of awareness, and candidates are hard pressed to make their cases, because the media pays little attention to issues. Further, in a state as large as Texas, the cost of advertising is almost prohibitive. In these races, endorsements by newspapers, bar groups (for judges), and other screening associations can be very important. A wise candidate seeks the recommendation of a group which agrees with his viewpoints. This can be crucial in a close race and illustrates again the importance of each individual vote.

Much attention is given to the major races for governor, lieutenant governor, attorney general, senator, etc., and issues are more clearly defined, although never to the degree that they should be. These races normally have the more expensive consultants and the capability to conduct frequent voter polls. The lack of true sophistication in politics is amazing. Most people who read a newspaper's poll accept it as being the absolute truth. Pre-election polls can vary widely, because the real issue is who will vote. Which groups have enough at stake to actually turn out? For that reason, the only valid poll is the election itself, and that occurs as a snapshot of public opinion on a certain day.

Public opinion normally varies back and forth and timing is important. Each campaign manager knows the key to victory is to have the candidate at his peak on election day. Public opinion polls taken six months before an election can indicate a weakness and opportunities to be exploited, but these cannot accurately predict the final outcome.

The media has begun to note that polls are more like weathervanes than compasses. They indicate what the public thinks now, but not what they will think in the future. This can present a problem to a politician who puts all his faith in polls and professional advice. The politician tends to look to the polls to see what the people think and want. In many cases, he does not realize that the movement of public opinion is often significantly slower than the movement of political events. It just takes much longer than people expect. The candidate has to inform, persuade and arouse multitudes. By the time that is accomplished, newer events are on center stage.

The fact that politicans look so closely to polls shows that they are not inclined to go against the public opinion. The statesman who makes the intelligent choice will often find that the public comes to appreciate his wisdom. This often requires not only faith in the people, but also an overriding willingness to choose the right direction.

Ronald Reagan's style has exemplified the challenge of standing one's ground in the face of negative public opinion. During the hail of media criticism focused on his Bittenberg trip and stance on South Africa, he stood firm. As a result, many of the people who didn't agree with Reagan respected and trusted him for being principled and leading with a "steady rudder" rather than fluctuating for convenience. Such a straightforward approach creates havoc in the world of politics today where everything is "professionalized." For the same reasons his actions in relation to the Iranian arms shipment caused severe repercussions, because this trust more than his judgement was put to question. Columnist Scott Bennett points out that the best swordsman in France never feared the second best swordsman. But he was terrified of the amateur who knew no real fear and whom the swordsman could not predict. Such is the power of candor and steadfastness in politics today.

One must also understand the logic behind the polls. The method used, the people questioned, and the questions asked are critical to the final result. Even if your candidate's poll shows him to be running ahead of the opponents, this might apply to only one or two categories. For example, in a particular gubernatorial election, three separate polls were taken, and all three candidates were extremely happy with the results. One had been interested in name identification, and he led the others by a great percentage. Another was pleased because he had surpassed his opponent in an overall poll, while the third candidate's poll showed him significantly ahead of the second. All were supposedly accurate and probably were. Unfortunately, they were comparing apples and oranges. Name identification polls oftentimes don't measure ideological differences, they only report who has heard of each candidate. The results are not necessarily the same when candidates are compared in a matched set of questions. The questions themselves can be biased and leading. Oftentimes, word identifications are included with the best polls so people can get more accurate readings of how the research should be interpreted.

Equally important, as in the above example, the poll should be relevant to the race being run. If one candidate's poll questions only Republicans, and his opponent queries all voters statewide, the statewide poll might well show that candidate to have a substantial lead if he was strong in the rural area, but many of these people would vote Democratic and therefore wouldn't be a factor in the Republican primary. So even if the poll was accurate, it would not be extremely relevant.

Additionally, if we look at polls separating Republicans and Democrats, we need to further refine the analysis by whether or not the respondents voted in perhaps the last two elections. Many people will give a party and a preference, but if they are not committed enough to vote, it really doesn't matter. This is referred to as "voter qualifications."

Many pollsters are increasingly refined and sophisticated in their methodology. They qualify the respondents by the fact that they voted in the last two or three elections and intend to vote in this one. The more accurate the definition, the more aspects of truth that can emerge. Circumstances and the issues of the day may bring a much larger turnout, and the polls will have overqualified the likely voters and missed other groups that will vote. So regardless of the surface accuracy of a poll, it needs to be examined carefully for what it really reveals about a particular point in time. It provides information about your present condition, but it doesn't necessarily tell you if you're getting better or worse.

It therefore becomes important to take a series of polls, just like thermometer readings, to show trends and directions. These can help identify what's causing the "illness" and what counter-measures are having any success by asking the right questions. Candidates and office holders who can afford these "trailing polls" receive a great amount of information not just about the candidate, but also on what people think about the issues of the day. If enough people favor an issue, you generally will see a politician charging out in front trying to lead the crowd in order to gain proper exposure. The polls are more helpful in informing voters about who is potentially winning or losing than in indicating a comprehension of ideas. Too many people see a poll and don't care enough about politics to do anything but vote for the likely winner. Or, if a candidate is not doing well, rather than helping him by increasing their support, voters may shrink back in fear of non-conformance. Polls always affect fundraising.

Many times political polls predict that a particular candidate will win. After the election, that same candidate and his supporters may sit and gaze dejectedly at the unopened champagne bottles standing in mockery of their premature glee. What the poll didn't explain was that who votes is as important as how they vote. For example, in a particular Texas election for governor, some polls showed that the incumbent was 7 to 8 percent ahead of his opponent the night before the election. Unfortunately, the poll only took into consideration voters who had voted in the last two elections and intended to again. But times had changed in Texas. We were experiencing an economic recession, and there was a tremendous voter turnout in many minority areas. A lot of these people had not voted in other elections, and so they had not been considered in the poll. At the same time, many of the candidate's supporters believed he would win by a large margin. They did not even bother to vote. Those two events combined to make a significant swing in that election.

Campaign organizations are almost never the well-oiled machines portrayed in the media and the movies, unless there is an overabundance of money. And generally if there is abundant money, people are tempted to spend it, which usually creates more problems than it helps. It takes a certain base amount of funding for each type of race. Once a certain expense level and organization has been achieved, the candidate, his ideas and the circumstances of the day begin to affect success. If a campaign does not have enough money, it is never able to reach that critical plateau to get name identification and exposure.

Funding becomes one of the primary concerns of any campaign and the major concern in Texas because of its size and numerous media markets. A state like Vermont or New Hampshire requires a very different strategy than a huge state like Texas, so funds can be allocated differently. In Texas money has to be committed to the various regional media markets, first to establish name identification and then to build the candidate's image.

In a Republican primary, there are nine, largely-metropolitan, areas where almost all money must be concentrated because that often is where the great majority of the Republican vote will be found for the primary. So even in spending the money carefully, the object is to obtain a weighted average of maximum cost benefit. This is very different from the politics of Dad's day, when people rode railroad trains and worked through the political party networks to gain name identification. Each individual now makes his own decisions with much less direction from party associates.

Every campaign has a private back room where strategy is planned. Generally the back room headquarters is staffed by only five or six key individuals such as:

(1) a campaign manager who tries to direct overall strategy, since a candidate literally has limited time and usually a biased perspective. The campaign manager generally will work with the specifics—polling, media, telephone banks, etc.

(2) a traveling aide who keeps the candidate on schedule for six or eight meetings and events in a day and who usually keeps track that all "in kind" contributions, such as receptions and so forth, are properly reported,

(3) a deputy campaign director who handles much of the day-to-day organization, while the campaign manager works with volunteers, fundraisers, and specialists such as media advisers,

(4) an issues coordinator who coordinates a policy committee to come up with ideas and positions,

(5) a press aide who must make sure messages are distributed and understood,

(6) county coordinators who establish an organizational structure. The political organization is composed largely of volunteer effort. Unfortunately, competent people who take an interest in politics are a rare commodity. No one ever realizes how difficult it is to have yard signs distributed, bumper stickers mailed, or even envelopes sealed, when you are dealing with hundreds of thousands of items. This need makes special interest groups particularly valuable because they can provide the manpower. The average person who gets involved in campaigns multiplies his vote as a result of his contribution.

The candidate is important. But quite frankly, he is in such a fast-moving and fast-paced world that the organization has to operate on its own. He normally spends a great amount of time trying to raise money to cover the ever-increasing budget, rather than thinking of strategy or issues. He may have hired direct mail specialists or fundraising experts but they, too, are costly, and the bigger contributors normally only respond to the personal touch. This need for funds often does not end even after the election, because he has to raise more money to keep a political organization in place for the next election. That is one of the unfortunate realities of modern media politics.

Too often, the candidate is surrounded by close associates with each vying for his personal attention. Dad once pointed out that the best thing you can do for your candidate is to find out what he needs—do it—and then talk to others on his behalf. If you are talking to him, you're occupying his time and your own, both of which could be spent getting additional votes; so have faith in the candidate and don't demand personal attention. The people most appreciated by a candidate are those who contribute funds at the very first when it is needed, perhaps before he appears to be a winner, and those who perform rather than talk.

Brilliant campaign strategies are often like programs implemented by government. Those that succeed are claimed; those that fail were someone else's idea. Some campaign managers appear brilliant because their candidate wins, but over a period of time, they have their losses as well. The political climate is a major factor in determining a winner or loser, and the candidate himself—his image, his depth, his financial backing—probably have much more to do with success than any grand strategy. The candidate usually wins by the normal slugfest of organization versus organization. The exception occurs when a candidate finds a single issue around which he can rally support at the right time and turn the campaign into a philosophical or ideological battle.

A campaign is designed, first and foremost, to sell a candidate to the people in the best light. That means he will agree normally to whatever the polls indicate the people want him to say, so skepticism is warranted and an in-depth look is required. Likewise, skepticism should be applied to negative campaigns where the only emphasis is to tear the other candidate down. These are far too common, because hate is a strong emotion that can be used extremely effectively. It is well to remember that if a candidate is focusing negatively on his opponent, it is usually because he does not wish to compare ideas. All campaigns, even those of statesmen, involve some negative aspects. Normally it is a defensive posture to point out facts opponents ignore. But generally statesmen emphasize why you should vote for them in a positive tone, not why you should vote against their opponents. That observation itself can tell you much about whom you should support if you wish to make a positive change in society. The nature and tenor of a campaign reveals a great deal about everyone involved in it.

There are few people who give money just for the purpose of improving government. Mainly, that's because they're not drawn into the political system. Far too often, it is easier to raise money for politics where people want access. It is not quite so easy, but still possible to raise money for the arts and humanities where people think they will get recognition. It is exceedingly difficult to raise money for objective research on issues such as education. If people do not see personal benefit either socially or financially, they often do not get involved within the process. They may be fickle and judge their every step by this criteria. They may talk of statesmanship and honor, and while some people are sincere, the majority of society is governed by a perception of personal advantage and selfish interest. So the few who do good for positive and unselfish reasons can have major impact, because they emerge from the crowd as cream does from milk.

Dad always said that if we want to get into politics, we should decide what we are going to do and then work extremely hard at it. Sometimes you encounter a race between two friends, and you may hesitate to get involved—either because of the friendship or sometimes because of uncertainty about who will win.

If you are asked to help by either side, there will be pressure placed upon you. Dad's philosophy "to make your choice based on the principles involved" was right, but the other side will inevitably say, "You just shouldn't work as hard as you could." That presents a two-fold problem. If there is a good reason for supporting one candidate, then you owe him your full backing. Secondly, if you give your full effort, you at least will be respected, and you will be among the first the other side will try to reconvert. Machiavelli perhaps said it best: "A neutral prince is respected by no one." If you wish to be considered a player in politics, you have to be a player. You can stay out and still be friends with all sides, but each candidate has an inner circle of supporters and workers who were there from the beginning. They have paid their dues, and thus are the people who are the most important and have the most say within an administration. Quite often, a person commits in response to the first request. That may not necessarily be the best person or strategy. Look to the other possible candidates and implication of the race. Prudence and wisdom in hesitating may enhance your image. The most prized converts are those who must be convinced.

It is equally true that to succeed in politics, you and the candidate have to understand how the system works in order to counteract it. A good candidate does not always win. History has shown that. "Right" does not always defeat "might". So it becomes extremely important for a candidate to be knowledgeable. He needs to understand and use media tactics and techniques. The major benefit for a good candidate is that people support him because of his principles—to a great extent they support his principles more than him.

Many people who get elected by putting together coalitions and making grand promises find that they cannot keep all of those promises. That loss of credibility can hurt not only them, but you as well if you make recommendations and unkept promises in their behalf. Advisors and strategists of savvy intelligence are a candidate's most valuable assets. There are people within politics who are referred to as "diamond cutters," because while you can randomly hit a diamond with a hammer and have no effect, if you strike at the right cleavage, it can be shattered with one stroke. An opponent's politics normally has many areas of cleavage, if they can be recognized. Coalitions brought together can often be separated by a simple examination of the facts, if a counter-campaign is intellectually organized. But ideals are slightly more difficult to attack, and quite often the strength of a candidate's winning margin is based on who is for him, not who is against him.

There are basically three types of people who get involved in a campaign:

(1) those who support a candidate's ideals,

(2) those who expect to benefit from his election,

(3) those who are against his opponent.

The latter two will provide help, but the real foundation for a successful campaign lies with those who believe in the candidate and his philosophy. Positive campaigners offering constructive solutions make long-term commitments more often than those who hate or dislike other candidates. Foundations can be built on rock or shifting sand.

Over an extended time, when a candidate follows his heart, principles, and ethics, he will find there are times he wins and times he loses; times he is in and times when he's out. If you are active when a candidate is in, then you are part of the inner circle and can actively affect policy, rather than being a outsider making suggestions. When your candidate is out, you are the loyal opposition. Constructive suggestions normally will be accepted because whoever is in government will want to be successful and remain in power. I have been condemned often by friends who feel it is improper to give good ideas to the opposition, because the opposition will take credit for them. But the real object of any involvement in the governmental process is to see that the best is done for the state and the nation. Politics is important, but it does not override your responsibility to support the opposition when they are right. This is not a concept of martyrdom, because eventually all sides recognize that you have integrity. Then in times of difficulty when all sides are divided and chopping at each other, you will have greater access to government because of your ability to work with all people as you have in the past. A reputation for fairness, intelligence and integrity can be the best way to advance ideals.

In summary, all elections differ. Some are philosophical, others are organizational; and sometimes fate determines a winner if economic or distant political events take an unexpected turn during a campaign.

It is important, however, to recognize the difference. In politics, organization and philosophy are like offense and defense in football. They are both present, but may be emphasized differently and need a combined and balanced strategy to be truly successful. In politics, this is similar to war strategies. In the past decades, political philosophy in China was dominated by Mao and his cultural revolution by which he changed the entire face of culture and belief in China for a period of time. It was an amazing transition, particularly since it was not that progressive. Now the reverse is occurring, which has incredible potential consequences for world history and economics.

What it teaches us is the eastern approach to the importance of thought. In our fast-paced western world, we have lost our focus on the power of ideas. Eastern people still possess that understanding, and it was used adeptly during the Vietnam War. When I was in the Navy, we studied the philosophies of war and military history from Rommel back to Thomas "Stonewall" Jackson to Karl von Clausewitz who studied Napoleon in an effort to defeat him. Von Clausewitz was an expert in tactics, troop concentrations, supply systems, and the fundamentals by which a "logistics war" was fought. It is very similar to today's political campaigns that rely on organization and large amounts of money, name identification, media, and billboards. Our nation was trained in the von Clausewitz style of war as we entered Vietnam. It was a winning strategy in World War II in the deserts of Africa and the battlefields of Europe.

In Vietnam, however, we encountered guerilla warfare similar to what Mao had used in China during World War II. His strategy was based on time, space, and thought: let the enemy expand over space; give him time to create discontent; and turn public opinion against him. A guerilla without the people's support would be a fish out of water. The keystone of Mao's success, however, was his ability to control ideas and get people to sacrifice through a massive change of philosophy. Mao knew that ideas are like hurricanes. They have tremendous power, although we can't always see them. They can build or defeat the national will and change a country's character and destiny.

Ideas can form and change both nations and local communities. Our politics move back and forth between these two styles of war, or in reality, styles of politics: the organizational method of tactics and the philosophical magnetism of ideas. In 1982, Texas' Democratic Party won a significant victory in all statewide offices. In large part, it was not a philosophical campaign at all. It was a campaign of turnouts, and they turned out their supporters extremely well through phone banks and organizational activities which they had not done in the past. People were concerned about the economy, and they voted according to their immediate needs. Few issues were discussed, and because it was an off year for the presidential campaign, little philosophy was involved. On the other hand, Ronald Reagan's elections in 1980 and 1984 were based on a philosophical approach. We perceived him to be a man of change; a conservative who would change direction, help get us back on a responsible path, and set the tone of the ticket.

Races vary with issues and time. However, by understanding both organizational and philosophical strategy, we can get a better perspective on campaigns. If we want to make wise decisions when voting, the best technique at our command is to look at the candidate, his principles, and his staff and supporters. Often we can learn more about a candidate by seeing a list of his supporters and endorsements than by listening to his speeches. It's also revealing to look at a list of the earliest supporters. These are the people who really believed in the candidate and took a financial and personal risk to support him. This list can tell you the ideology behind the candidate which encouraged him to run in the first place. People who become supporters later in the race or when he's running for a second term are less reliable indicators of his true beliefs. Those people are supporting him primarily because they want to make sure they're on the winner's side. The campaign's style, whether it is dirty or clean, the intelligence of the candidate's statements, and his willingness to talk about issues say more than an expensive advertisement on the television or in the newspapers.

Another focus of a campaign is the human being who has decided to run for office. It's easy to criticize a politician without understanding some of the sacrifices and difficulties he has to endure. A candidate's life is very difficult today. Opponents and the media look into every corner of his life. Even if skeletons aren't found in his closets, opponents, separate interest groups, or a small sensationalistic group of journalists can usually cast some sort of doubt on his integrity or lifestyle. Allegation and innuendo too often replace fact. The cost of campaigning is immense. A recent candidate for Governor of Texas spent an estimated $13 million during one election. If a person isn't independently wealthy, raising money or paying back campaign debts can become huge burdens, particularly if he has a family to support. Campaigning and being in the political realm is a tough lifestyle that most of us can't comprehend simply by watching television or reading the papers.

Today's political lifestyle is incredibly different from Jefferson and Lincoln's time. Times were slower, and issues were far less complex; there was more time for deliberation. Now politics is a fast-moving and time consuming occupation. When someone contemplates running for office, he has to think about how the decision will affect every aspect of his life. One of the first considerations is his family. Those people closest to a candidate or politician inevitably suffer, because there's simply no way to do a good job for a large constituency and still spend quality time with a spouse or children. This is particularly true with statewide or national offices. The candidate is committed to a frenetic schedule of running for election and making frequent tours of his district. His time is limited.

A congressional or senate seat in Washington requires tremendous commitment. With large constituencies, many of whom want personal service, a politician's day becomes a succession of short telephone calls, meetings, and letters, plus directing staff. At least 50 percent of his time is consumed with correspondence and raising money.

Dad often said that there are usually two tears for every smile in politics. Even if a politician makes a good decision that will help many people, he will still make enemies because certain individuals didn't get everything they wanted. I remember one politician saying that it seemed whenever he took any action, he had to smooth over somebody's feelings. A governor soon finds for every person he appoints, 20 are rejected and upset and will remember him negatively. The one selected usually feels he deserved it and isn't that much more supportive. Power is not always positive.

In Texas, elections have become extremely expensive. A congressional race in Texas easily can cost between$400,000 and $500,000; a senatorial race between $8 and $9 million; a gubernatorial primary, perhaps $ 3.5 million; and a gubernatorial election between $10 and $12 million. In some metropolitan markets, one 30-second television spot can cost $25,000. That means non-stop fundraising to reduce debts and accumulate enough to keep campaign committees working. These financial burdens greatly limit our choices, as fundraising becomes a major determinant of candidate availability. Many good men or women may be interested in an office, but we can only vote for those on the ballot, and fundraising speaks to who is there.

Some of us see political action committees (PAC's) as weapons used by business and labor to influence and intimidate members of Congress. That simply is not the reality of political financing in today's world. Most political action committees are inundated with literature and phone calls from legislators and congressmen, because they are the candidates who need to raise large amounts of money. In many districts, re-election costs often exceed the amount of political money available from local sources. This means that money has to be solicited from almost all political action committees.

If you attend political receptions or dinners, you simply sit at a dinner, listen to the speakers, and enjoy the applause and ceremony. Most of us seldom realize that the candidate is probably counting the tables to see how many finally were sold in order to have an idea of where he stands in regard to his cash flow. If a candidate loses the election, he is responsible for paying off whatever debt remains if he wishes to run again in the future, and he is often personally liable for a good part of it. A $500,000 deficit is discouraging, since people normally contribute money to the winner who can be of help to them. They seldom give to a loser or help him pay that deficit. That is when a person discovers his true friends. Unfortunately, true friendship is rare.

Unfortunately, deficits are far more common than most people realize. Many times, a candidate personally guarantees campaign loans because the money is needed to run crucial last-minute media spots. He does that on a gamble that he'll win and be able to raise the money later. The problem occurs if he loses. Losses can then affect the financial and personal lives of candidates and their closest friends who are usually asked to guarantee campaign notes as well. Intent upon winning, many candidates just don't think about this problem and figure the money will come in some way. Other people decide not to run because of this potential financial burden. A large deficit may convince the candidate to take a "double or nothing" position and run again as soon as possible to help raise money. It is a combination of these fears, more than greed, that makes many legislators build large, and apparently unneeded, war chests in advance of a campaign.

Real friends in politics are a rare commodity. Most people who pose as friends have a personal stake in wanting to see a person become a representative or governor. However, these people take very little risk.

Friends who urge a person to run for office obviously have a different perspective and degree of commitment. Dad often repeated the old political saying that when a person is considering running for office, his breakfast of bacon and eggs should remind him that there is a difference between involvement and commitment. The chicken was involved in providing the breakfast, but the pig was committed.

Dad also noted that if one gets heavily involved in local politics such as a school board race, he should understand at the start that principle has its reward and its price, and he needs to think about Travis at the Alamo. Even if he wins and is able to act on his principles, he will face opposition and criticism. It is the candidate who must face the potential deficits and commit six to nine months for campaigning at the expense of family, business, and all other enjoyable activities. The candidate's entire focus will be on running for election, meeting people, shaking hands, building records, building files, and building organizations. All for a job that basically pays very little.

Every individual has true friends who believe in him and his ideals. As a result, they will often work long and hard hours. But because they are such close friends, a candidate has to be concerned about them also. By getting involved in a hopeless race, he can do himself and his friends a disservice. They may have to turn down other requests for support, and they will probably make enemies by backing him. If he loses the race, they might be branded as having opposed the winner, which could negatively affect them during an incumbent's entire term. The more prominent they are, the more cheap shots will be taken if the winner is political in nature and has not yet learned that intimidation and revenge only breed problems as the cycle turns.

When a candidate runs, he has a responsibility to win. The best leaders ask people to commit to ideals rather than an individual. Even friends feel better about supporting a set of concepts. That's why a candidate needs to know whether he is running for a cause or for his own personal satisfaction. If he's running for ego gratification, he needs to be even more certain he can win before asking his friends to risk their time, money, and reputations. Before making a commitment, every potential supporter, whether a close friend or casual acquaintance, should make sure he knows why a person wants to run for political office.

If, as a friend, you actively encourage someone to run when his chances for winning are very slim, you can lose more than you may realize. Some politicians believe that if they lose, no one else will be hurt. That is never the case. Ideals can be damaged if a candidate loses a race without representing those principles adequately. The money that was raised could have gone to another candidate with similar ideals who might have won.

Once candidates get elected, they are thrown into a new political game with different rules. If you are trying to get a law changed or a new law passed, you'll be working with politicians in an entirely different way than what you did during campaign time. That's the world of legislative politics.

Legislative politics is more private than electoral politics. During a campaign, we are bombarded by discussion of issues and debates on policy through television and newspapers. On the other hand, we can read about the debate and passage of bills in the legislature, but we don't get to see what compromises had to be made and why certain portions of bills failed to be included for the final vote. Political trade-offs usually are kept quiet, because the spirit of compromise allows the legislature to work. It takes our representatives long enough to pass needed legislation. If no one were willing to compromise, we would probably still be sitting in Philadelphia debating the Declaration of Independence. Yet we always face the dilemma of conscience versus convenience and short-term benefits versus long-term goals that each leader can only decide for himself. However, a leader's character is usually an indication of his direction. His long-term record will speak for itself, if we take the time to look into it.

The committee, advisory group or other similar body is a key vehicle of legislative politics. This style relies greatly on procedural approaches to centralize power in positions. Any committee or study group can be a vehicle to bring about consensus or can be used to kill an issue. The true motivation in forming such a group is the most accurate prediction of its impact.

It is important to understand that bargaining needs to take place, and we should judge our leaders by how well they have negotiated and stood by their principles. Just because a representative says he voted for a bill does not necessarily mean that he has served us well. Unless a piece of legislation is built on a set of principles to accomplish a specific end, it may do more harm than good. Too often, a bill is just an expedient fix during a period of intense emotional interest in a single issue. The focus on such an issue only lasts for a limited amount of time, and anything that substitutes for action can often quiet the public.

Maybe you've heard the apocryphal story of the strawberry short-cake bill, an example of legislation made without a guiding set of ideas or principles. A bill was introduced to make strawberry shortcake the "official state dessert." A detailed explanation defined each ingredient such as flour, sugar, cream and strawberries, but after the bill was amended, a strawberry shortcake emerged that used cornmeal, salt, buttermilk and sliced radishes. It was proclaimed a strawberry shortcake, but nothing from the original bill was left. Tourists who ate the "official dessert" probably thought that the residents of that state were crazy. Though testimonials proclaimed this to be one of the delicacies of all mankind, it tasted awful.

As in the strawberry shortcake story, many good and sometimes great ideas are introduced as bills in the legislature. Legislators and outside experts give testimony to support those ideas. However, as everyone gets an opportunity to add his own special touch, the great idea loses much of its initial value. The original concept becomes an empty shell which is carefully retained only to make sure the bill is passed. The purpose has been obscured, and the end product ends up helping only a few special interest groups. In the strawberry shortcake example, the bottom-line benefit was for radish farmers. Unfortunately, few people get the opportunity to see the motivation influencing the outcome. They only know it doesn't taste good; so they assume the original idea was bad.

We should remember in trying to analyze legislation that there are two main divisions or types. One relates to economic redistribution and growth. The other deals with what I consider to be moral principles, including crime and punishment. For consistency, both politicians and individuals need to have defined goals in each area.

Politicians also practice a form of persuasion called positioning. This occurs when a legislator performs an apparently noble act which is actually a disguise for accomplishing a political objective. A skillful legislative strategist picks issues and tries to clothe them in righteousness. Based on the result he wants to achieve, he finds out what the public thinks should be done and what noble cause they will support. Armed with that information, the legislator dresses his bill in the nobility and morality that his poll tells him people will applaud. He appears righteous, and most people will praise his high-mindedness. This clears the way for easier passage of the real legislation, which is not always what we think we are getting. It also makes coming home to his constituents a happy and peaceful event, and it helps cement the next election.

A typical example is the politician in a very religious community who passes legislation eliminating liquor purchases on credit in an effort to cut down drunkenness. This leaves the impression that he is standing up for sobriety. In reality, the liquor industry, which has been lobbying him also, is ecstatic, because now they have an excellent reason not to provide credit, which helps their business. The bill accomplishes two ends and keeps both sides of the politician's constituency happy.

Legislators sometimes resort to positioning, because so many people are resistant to change. We also resent legislation being pushed through the democratic process by brute force. Change frightens a lot of us, since experience has taught us that new, ill-bred laws more often harm than harm us. A legislator who is anxious to gain support for his legislation doesn't want to stir up unnecessary resistance, so he uses the power of right where possible. It's more effective and efficient in the long run. The objective is wrapped in a "righteousness" which suits most people's prejudices and opinions.

While it's difficult to sift through this manipulation, it becomes possible by developing a deeper understanding of issues and a broader perspective which helps us discern who will benefit monetarily or economically from passage of a bill. The root cause of much positioning is economic; it is unfortunate, but it is a reality. If you look hard enough at the financial beneficiaries of positioning, you'll have a better understanding of how good the bill is for society as a whole. I don't mean to imply that all legislation is based on economic motivation. Many non-economic bills also serve special interests. However, it is an excellent litmus test. To re-emphasize, there are really only two types of issues—social and economic—that come before a deliberative body. If we could separate the two, and discuss each on its merits, the answers would be simpler than now, when the issues are often strategically mixed.

The same concerns affect support for issues that promote the common good. I found this to be the case when I chaired an organization called Texans for Quality Education, Inc. It was an objective research group looking at the implementation of the major educational reforms. The board was composed of prominent business and professional figures, who favored an unquestioned strategic approach. This organization had the blessing of state officials, the media, and many educational groups. However, the very corporations that would give tens of thousands of dollars to candidates to run advertisements on behalf of education and stating their positions on the issue, often did not have $1,000 to give to objective research that might have actually dealt with the problems. I have raised great amounts of money for the arts, for politics, and for advocacy organizations. And it always amazes me how few people give, no matter how noble the cause, to activities that are truly aimed at the ultimate benefit of society, but don't offer a personal reward in publicity, financial gain, political access, or ego enhancement. There are, however, a limited few who truly care about long-term issues and do what they can to see that the right answers are chosen for the right reasons. This influence is greater than they expect, because objectivity is rare and respected in the political process.

A drawback in legislative politics is that public servants can become overly political. If they live in a city like Austin or Washington, where the majority of their associates are also politicians, they don't always get a true reading of their constituents back home. They normally work with lobbyists, trade association executives, their staff, and other elected officials. Media coverage is far more intense, which makes reading how issues are perceived by an average man more difficult. In Austin or Washington, people are surrounded by a social scene in which these various groups interact, creating personal relationships that can distort judgements. Politicians who return home more often can keep their finger on their constituents' wants and needs. If an official only visits the folks back home during election time, there can be a rude awakening on election day when he discovers that he has lost touch with his supporters.

In contrast, once an election is over, another is generally not faced for years. Thus, relationships in electoral politics are different than those in legislative politics, where there may be a thousand issues in one legislative session. Legislators may be enemies on one particular issue, but friends on another. It is not unusual for issues to bring odd groupings of people together. In electoral politics, politicians do not see supporters as often as they work with other legislators, and it's harder to repair bridges. Ill feelings often fester, given the very personal nature of politics, and a politician has to be particularly sensitive to the aftermath of an election. Many a politician has come to regret not extending a friendly hand after a victory. A statesman realizes he needs and must seek the support of all to govern well. Dad believed that humility was a major virtue in politics. In legislative politics, divisions tend to be more philosophical, feelings are smoothed over out of necessity, and a congenial working relationship is developed. That is not usually possible in electoral politics, where people are seldom seen and jagged edges often remain.

When people think of legislative politics, the image of a cigar-smoking, smooth-talking, well-paid individual may come to mind. Often the connotation is that this person lacks a stable foundation of ethical principles. I believe that it is wrong to think of lobbyists as negative players, although this can be true in some circumstances. The nature of politics is changing because of the media's continuing interest in focusing light upon the activities that build legislation. In times past, where little attention was paid to the back room politics, personal friendships and campaign contributions played a significant role in what occurred. Being a part of the team was—and still is—critically important. But Texas leadership in Austin, while very powerful, now emphasizes coordination of interests as a tool rather than the power politics of the past.

Part of this has come about because of the state's rapid transition from a rural to an urban-dominated legislature. The Republican party has also become a major force, and the public has paid much more attention to political style. Recognizing the importance of the media, lobbyists are concentrating more on facts and substantive arguments. The lobby now understands that success will come from arguing on the basis of right rather than might. Money is useful to gain access, but it is readily available from various sources. No one group dominates the halls of Congress or the legislature. Therefore, candidates try to align with the sources that most represent their constituents, because they are as concerned about elections and issues as they are about money. Lobbyists can provide a candidate with more substantial and detailed information on an issue than might otherwise be available to him. It is important, however, that the candidate listen to both sides of the issue while recognizing the direction and orientation of the lobbyist.

Generally, lobbyists either represent a standing constituency on a long-term basis and are very familiar with specific issues, or they are "free lance lobbyists"—often referred to as "gun slingers." These people are hired for specific purposes because of their expertise in putting together coalitions, their access to key figures, or their intricate knowledge of the system. Lobbyists are neither good nor bad as a group. Their efforts can be beneficial or harmful. It depends on the position they take and its effect on the overall system. Lobbyists represent their clients' interest, and they have a right to be heard. The problem with this system, some say, is that groups economically unable to hire a lobbyist are not represented. But consumer-oriented groups and the substantial voting base of the average man provide a more significant counterbalance than most people realize.

As stated earlier, lobbyists can provide important information on issues. When a decision is made solely on that basis, not for personal reasons, and not related to contributions, lobbyists can be extremely helpful. The lobbyists divide along unique lines be they conventionally-retained or independents. I have seen some lobbyists devote many hours of private time to areas such as the Texas Lyceum and education. They have helped raise money and support for organizations that furthered the common good rather than any personal benefit. Other lobbyists greatly resent and feel threatened by my brand of philosophy, which encourages people to become knowledgeable and able to exercise personal power in the public process.

I have found it beneficial to encourage corporate and legislative leaders to talk about matters directly rather than through lobbyists. It promotes a sharper focus upon the respective needs when discussion is not filtered through the lobby process. But the lobby itself is neither right nor wrong, good nor bad. It is an institution that performs a certain function within a democracy. Its members are motivated by self-interest—and in some cases, by a desire for good public policy. Lobbyists will never be eliminated, but when the process is conducted openly, there is a better chance that good policy will be supported for the right reasons. In these complex times, they often play an essential part in the process by expediting legislation.

Normally, a lobbyist is retained by a trade association, whose executive director has considerable influence based on his knowledge of the process. Trade associations provide much information to legislators and to the general public as well. They are a key link in representing the people.

These organizations play an important part in developing ideas and building a national will. In the early days of Texas, the chambers of commerce were unifying organizations for the common good. The motto of the earliest chamber in New York was a Latin phrase, translated: "Not Born for Ourselves Alone." In Texas, the four regional organizations, the East Texas, West Texas, South Texas and Rio Grande Valley Chambers, backed issues from agricultural advancement to the farm-to-market road system. They helped start universities and supported education. As times became more sophisticated and tax policy grew more important, other groups logically bonded together to represent the interests of bankers, doctors, and individual industries.

Later, associations of individual industries organized larger support bases until there were divisions within an industry, such as banking, separating the independent banks and the holding companies. As a result, a myriad of forces began to affect the legislature. Rather than being a single group for the common good, they became simply many special interest groups, each concerned with its own basic welfare. At the same time, the political parties changed by adding caucuses and looked more to special interests than politics. Much of this related back to the Depression, when the income tax philosophy was changed from raising money to rewarding and punishing different types of economic activities for social purposes, such as liberalized depreciation allowances that might benefit real estate interests or heavy excise taxes on liquor that might decrease alcohol consumption.

America had a comfortable economic margin after World War II. Our independence from the rest of the world allowed us to change internal policy to try to reach specific ends with much less difficulty than is now the case, when we have limited margin and significant international activity and competition. To use Texas as an example, since Washington parallels it very closely, additional non-profit organizations have formed in the last 20 years which are playing increasingly important roles in finding rational solutions to perplexing questions. These groups have responded to our need for independent analysis of our problems from an objective viewpoint. They are categorized under the Internal Revenue Service Code as educational, religious, and charitable organizations plus various other groups that can do policy research under IRS Section 501(C)(3).

The premier organization of this nature in our state is the Texas Research League, Inc., which has completed political studies on governmental programs and provided beneficial research and analytical material. The League does not take political positions on issues, does not endorse candidates, and scrupulously avoids any political overtone. Thus it has the ability to accept contributions from almost all sources. A slightly different style of organization formed in recent years is the Texas Lyceum Association, Inc., which serves as a catalyst to bring together many similar groups for a comprehensive overview of the state and other purposes. Texans For Quality Education, Inc. assisted in monitoring the effects of changes in the education field. In recent years an increasing number of university-related think tanks have been established, such as the Institute of Constructive Capitalism founded by George Kozmetsky at the University of Texas at Austin and similar major efforts in studies at almost all of the Southwest Conference schools. This is a new and positive phenomenon, since it is a Texas response to the state problems and a movement toward the generation of "third coast" ideas and solutions.

It is remarkable that most of these institutes have been able to work in close coordination, so that their research was not wasted. Instead, the programs have been well-orchestrated and jointly developed. Perhaps the greatest unseen benefit of the Texas Lyceum Association, Inc. has been its efforts to serve as a catalyst in pulling together the best minds for joint programs as it allows all of these groups to work together, avoiding duplication and focusing on needs. This research think-tank approach is the best example of Texas' increasing academic sophistication. A current target is to evolve strategies and technologies for reducing our oil dependence. Though Texans are famous for our internal resolve, that characteristic becomes immaterial, if we do not have a strategic and practical game plan. Determination without vision is an emotional shadow of true strength.

Another type of organization is similar in form to a chamber of commerce, and though it has limitations on what it can do within the political sector, it can play a more active part in actually working with legislation. According to the Internal Revenue Service Code, these organizations are distinguished by the fact that they are able to influence the political process. A good example is the Texas Association of Taxpayers, Inc. It has done the state a great amount of good by providing expert analysis and alternatives on tax policy. Organizations such as this can receive corporate support, but are not in a charitable category as were the previously mentioned organizations. Their involvement in electoral politics is limited by the Internal Revenue Code.

Another group of organizations are known as Political Action Committees (PACs). The funds donated to them are not tax-deductible. Corporations cannot fund PACs except through their officers and other employees or individuals who are able to make the contributions. These are pure political dollars that go to candidates. PACs are normally organized on a state basis for state races and on a federal basis for federal races. State and federal laws for contributions are different. The federal law sets out distinct limitations which are strictly enforced.

The Political Action Committees themselves have become as divided as the trade associations. There are several statewide PACs that are interested in good government. They raise money on an organized basis and give to the most qualified people. There are innumerable independent company, union, and trade association Political Action Committees that give money to support their respective issues, but problems occur when you focus on just one issue. A person may vote for your interests on the issue of international trade, which may be critically important, but against your position in overall tax policy. By elevating single issues above general philosophies, more harm than good is done, to the point that more money does not necessarily equate with victory, once a base minimum is reached. This means that it is easy for candidates, who may not have major individual support, to pick up enough money to be competitive and get elected by using emotional rather than logical approaches.

As with lobbies, the impact of Political Action Committees depends on their motivation and whether they stand for an overall viewpoint, rather than representing only their individual interests. What we are finding in America is that while we fight over what remains of the pie, the pie tends to shrink if we do not look at the broader and more important strategies that make the pie grow larger for us all. The political networks, as described, play a major role, because they affect both electoral and legislative policies. We place many burdens upon our legislative representatives. We pay them relatively little, and we expect total personal service and communication. We are disappointed when we see how they spend their office-holder accounts. We expect high ethical standards—and rightly so, since they are in the public trust. But it is also important to understand the system before judging their actions.

State law allows almost unlimited contributions in Texas while federal law allows only a $1,000 maximum contribution from an individual to a candidate for election. The Texas approach of not limiting contributions from individuals has both benefits and detriments. It makes it easier for candidates to raise money, so they can get their messages to people, but it puts them in the difficult situation of owing at least a moral debt to contributors. Many would prefer that the law be changed, but the practical problem is the tremendous size of our state and the large number of media markets that must be covered. To run for office in Texas is extremely expensive, and there is strong feeling that we should not limit government only to those who can personally afford to participate. The media has done much to analyze where these support bases are, and the specter of unfavorable publicity provides some natural checks and balances. However, people need to be aware that Texans give money for good government, because they realize that it is an essential part of the economic climate. Just because a man makes a large contribution and is appointed to an office should not automatically carry negative implications. The question is whether he is the best appointment available. The political system always promotes friends, but it is also natural to choose people in whom you have confidence. It is improper to automatically assume conflict of interest. Too often that means you must choose someone who knows nothing about an issue rather than an honorable and knowledgeable man.

The flip side of the coin occurs when an official attempts to punish enemies by never considering them, even though they may be the best qualified, for appointment to an office. This is where he fails the state and nation. People vote for a man because they feel he is the best for them. He owes them the responsibility of assembling the best government possible. He has to be partisan and loyal to party where the characteristics of potential appointees are equal, but if one towers above the others in abilities and other considerations, I feel he has an obligation to build the best team possible. The point can be argued many ways, but the logic is still there.

Certainly, the best way to influence legislation is to win the support of the people. Trade associations are oriented toward selling their most popular viewpoints. Representatives will appear on the news talk shows, and some organizations will buy time on cable. Lobbyists will make presentations that allow the politicians excellent arguments for taking certain actions. Old style politics will inevitably remain, but the activities of these multiple groups will emphasize the importance of ideas and recognize an increasingly intelligent electorate. Tort Law reform is only one of the recent examples. The media will continue to play a significant role, because it will put forth the economic arguments and available choices. Media will shape the political process even more than before. The benefit may well be that people will not only need to look good on TV, but will have to be increasingly intelligent as well. People will expect political leaders to have a sophisticated and coordinated philosophy of government to present for consideration.

The bureaucracy is made up of government agencies and commissions. which are the continuing government, because they remain in Austin or Washington D.C. after the politicians have passed from the scene. Members of the bureaucracy change slowly, although the governor can affect this by appointments.

But as much good can be done by the legislature by their oversight and funding. The Lieutenant Governor, the Speaker of the Texas House, committee chairmen, and government agency heads can have visits or hearings. At those hearings, information may be produced on a new bill or serve another important purpose of reminding the agency director that he is tied into the legislative process and is accountable to the voters in a round-about way.

Unless he plays bureaucratic politics astutely, the agency director could end up with fewer employees, no money, or no agency at all under the sunset provisions. This tends to produce responsiveness. But the key to good government really lies in the quality of the governor's appointments to those agencies. These individuals can implement careful spending and enlightened policies, or they can merely show up for meetings to hear reports and drink coffee. A governor is responsible for making the best possible appointments to assure an intelligent and responsible government. We, therefore, have a right to expect more than partisan rewards as a decision criterion for those appointments. The governor should not just choose from those who seek a position. For critical positions that require expertise, ideas, or creativity, he should recruit the best possible people who truly can do an effective job. The most qualified candidates will probably be too busy to think about asking for an appointment, so he needs to go beyond the requests that appear over his desk.

Despite an understanding of how legislative politics works, some efforts at making changes in government may still fail, while others are successful in accomplishing goals. These people or groups often have exercised their power through the other branches of government when blocked in the legislative branch. The three branches of government exercise power in very different ways. The effective lobbyist knows how to work in each of the three branches and how to control the "power current" to achieve his or her objectives. All of us have to understand how to exercise power this way to effectively judge our leaders' motivations.

Power is distributed among the three branches of government. The legislative branch makes the laws and funds the agencies; the executive branch implements and enforces the laws; and the judicial branch interprets the laws. We memorized the names and basic duties of the three branches in school. But did we ever learn how to exercise self-government effectively within these realms? Lobbyists try to spread their influence in all three branches because they know that there are a variety of ways to affect legislative outcome. Therefore, we also need to understand the interrelationships of the three branches.

There are a number of ways in which public policy is made and enacted. Just because a bill is passed or rejected, that doesn't mean the end of a movement or idea. For example, if a law is passed which prohibits the dumping of toxic wastes on public lands, the bill's opponents may lobby the executive branch for limited enforcement. Opponents may also try to have broad exemptions, favorable to their position, passed along with the law. So although the bill becomes law, the lobbyists work with the executive branch to bend the legislation to help them. Similarly, electing candidates to the highest state courts who have particular leanings on issues can lead to future decisions that create a form of judicial law through court precedent. A Supreme Court ruling on an issue such as wrongful death can accomplish as much or more than a legislative bill. Therefore, an awareness of the judiciary and the judges' qualifications and backgrounds is equally important, if we are to express our own will. Too often these elections are dominated with money and support only by interested parties. The real importance and opportunity for an individual citizen to have additional input and power in the system is missed.

When we look at the patterns of history and see economic difficulties causing the grave hardships, we can see also that the people's character during those times determined their destiny. The character of a nation or state is evident in its devotion to ideals and moral values. And those values can be found in the economics and politics of a nation. People of high character are willing to sacrifice and build upon such ideals as freedom and opportunity—characteristics Texans have traditionally honored. People give ideas power because they are willing to sacrifice for them.

In the late 1960s, when I was attending the University of Texas, I arrived on campus at the height of the Vietnam protest activity. Somehow Austin had become the unofficial headquarters of noncomformist ideas. Since I attended the business school, I had a distinctly conformist viewpoint. During one of his visits to Austin, Dad was amazed at the dress, activism, and direction that my generation appeared to be moving in. Rebellion against authority opposed patriotism in his eyes. He expressed dismay that the country had forgotten the moral values he had taught me, because people were no longer concerned about each other. He watched them pursue their special interests and single issues, and he felt that the glue that held society together was gradually weakening. He feared that someday America would face what other societies had known and that eventually we'd have a dictatorship in response to growing anarchy. He saw institutions such as the family and religion becoming less of a guiding force. He often told me that history has been a succession of institutional authorities, each of which gradually weakens and loses the power to command the people's respect and loyalty.

In the early 1960s, Dad had seen nationalism arise with John Kennedy, the Cuban Missle Crisis, the space challenge, and economic innovations such as the tax cut and investment tax credit. These activities seemed to gain people's respect and encourage trust in government. But in the later 60s, he noted a declining interest in joining political parties and an erosion of patriotism. In Austin, he saw an opposition to the government that bordered on lawlessness. He recognized in the politics of that day the tactics of polling and positioning, the striving to say nothing convincingly and the conscious attempt to avoid real issues. He felt he had seen America already beyond its climax, for the system lacked leadership and intelligence. The younger and inexperienced generation wanted not simply to change the system, but to overthrow it. These people were willing to take a firm position, and he feared it. He once commented that the era of ideas seemed to be ending, and perhaps it was best that he had lived in an earlier time period. He regretted that his generation had not done more to leave the world in a better state for my generation to inherit.

Although those were difficult years, time has shown that some benefits resulted. Perhaps the rebellion and free-thinking of that generation may have led to the Reagan Revolution. The 1960s generation may have learned more about values than their parents realized. They were taught justice, and so they recognized injustice. They were better educated, and they understood the function of government and how it could be used to effect change. The radicalism of the 60s may have been an extreme exhibition of power as that new generation came of age. And perhaps Dad overlooked two of his favorite adages. The first was that for every action, there is a reaction that must be anticipated. The second was that the first 40 years of life provide the text by which we gain experience and understanding, and the next 30 years are the commentary, where we use that experience and our abilities to make a mark upon history. I believe that some members of the 60s generation will experience a rebirth in the late 1980s and 1990s and will return to a more mature participation in the governmental process. And we will all be better served. Dedication to ideas was present in the 1960s, although in a less familiar form.

The generation represented at the University of Texas at that time had to live through a difficult period. It fought in Vietnam. It suffered the worst ravages of inflation while trying to build its families, and it has faced a world of intense economic competition without the economic or military margins that preceding generations had known. It was an intelligent, educated, and resourceful generation that had a better understanding of the real values of life than critics might have expected. And today many of us wish to return to the order, the meaningful relationships, and the values that prevailed in the past. As this generation came of age, we became the dominant voting block in the country. Members of my generation still understand what government can do, but we have, more importantly, learned why economics is critically important. As our country faces choices, there is more appreciation for the importance of ideas. The "yuppies" of media acclaim may have peculiarities, but they are also much smarter, and I feel, considerably more socially concerned than the stereotype might indicate.

The children of the '60s knew government was the key institution to direct the economic and political environments as well as affecting the cultural and communications segments of society. I'm not sure, however, if they clearly appreciated their power in a democracy which relies on a unified national strength and moral will. What we now must understand is that our children will soon replace us, as they enter that questioning age. The world has become more complex, and we have less margin for error. We need a unified national will that will allow us to choose a direction. We need to decide on a national agenda and explain its importance to our children, if our generation is to merit their confidence and support.

The first priority in this positive style of government is to have a basic goal by which to judge direction and accomplishment. If we go back to the beginnings of recorded history, we find a document written by Aristotle called "Politics." In his mind, the purpose of government was to achieve the most good possible for the people. He believed that state leaders should be loyal to the state, competent in performing the duties of their offices, and should possess virtues, such as integrity and a sense of justice. He thought that the preservation of the state rested with the education of its citizens. Without education, Aristotle felt that even the wisest laws would be of little benefit. He held that man was a political animal, and the state was his creation, not something forced upon him.

To me, this has always been the proper view of the nature of a state or nation. It places the highest value upon the individual citizen and his greatest good. Generally, the most successful states have been those which had codes of conduct that worked for the good of all citizens. In history, those states have always gained increasing support for the common man. It is obvious that George Washington stands in a far nobler historic position than Adolph Hitler. And that position is not due to victory or defeat on the battleground.

As history moved forward from Aristotle, a countervailing idea emerged during the time of the Italian Medici family in Florence. It presented a nationalistic viewpoint that the state was the important agent of action and, sadly, people were to be considered inert objects to be moved at will by the state. This concept was vigorously expressed by Niccolo Machiavelli in his work, *The Prince*. Some might consider it unfair to characterize Machiavelli with the negatives of nationalism seen in the regimes of Mussolini, Hitler, and Stalin. Machiavelli wrote in an age when democracies, as we know them today, did not exist. People lived in principalities, and this influenced his thinking. It is more appropriate to visualize the monarchies of England and particularly France, where the output of a nation was directed not to its people, but to the King at Versailles. People might be severely wanting, but resources were managed according to his wishes, even if an orchard of orange trees had to be moved indoors every winter. Although Machiavelli's book has been read by many leaders on both sides of government philosophy, it is perhaps the most thorough work that argues for the importance of a state. To Machiavelli, the state was a force to be driven by its leadership. But there is no inherent purpose in any state. The ruler may guide it according to his own will and desires. As the late Dean Christian Gauss of Princeton so critically noted in his analysis, the people are seen as basically inert, and therefore their education and concerns are relatively unimportant.

Aristotle's *Politics* and Machiavelli's *The Prince* can give us insight into two major theories of government. The underlining distinction of those theories lies in the power given to the state as opposed to that accorded the people. In the course of history, St. Thomas Aquinas added morality to many of Aristotle's concepts. Still later, one of the fundamental thinkers in the American Revolution, Thomas Jefferson, was concerned with limiting state power. Nowhere in *The Prince* is any limit placed upon the state. Jefferson believed in a doctrine of inalienable rights of man. He supported basic human rights and equity.

If we believe in caring for the individual citizen and allowing the most freedom and education for people, I think we can see that nations and leaders who support these ideas figure among the more praise-worthy societies and figures in history. For example Confucius lived around 500 B.C. He preached loyalty, benevolent authority and duty toward authority, courtesy, moderation, and the golden social rule, "What you do not want done to yourself, do not do to others." Those fundamental principles established a religion and ethical code which has swayed the Chinese soul for centuries. At 22, Confucius began a career as a teacher and sage by starting an academy which taught these principles of conduct in government. At the age of 52, he was called to office in his native state and made governor of the City of Chaung-Tu. His wise administration garnered acclaim. Confucius improved communications and transportation. He fought crime. But while his policies were immensely popular with the people, he was opposed by the powerful interests and eventually sent into exile. His books were burned, only to be redeemed and taught in later times. When Confucius died in 476 B.C., he was a disappointed and disillusioned man of 73, unaware of the enduring power of his ideas. Men may die, but ideas can live forever. They can only be killed by other ideas.

The teachings of Christ illustrate the power of ideas in convincing people to sacrifice for what they deeply believe. There are examples throughout history of people as diverse as Mahatma Gandhi and Sir Thomas More, who have been devoted to an ideal. In Texas, there is no written communication more thrilling than Travis' last letter from the Alamo. It radiated the spirit of those Texans who stepped across the line he drew, knowing it meant almost certain death.

Yet to understand the problems of our government today, we still need to carry the concept of the importance of ideas one step further and understand how our nation arrived at its present stage of thinking. During the time Jefferson was writing about individual rights of man, three philosophies of government were influential.

The first of these was liberalism, which emphasizes a free individual and opposes oppressive control by institutions. It was best conveyed in the writings of John Locke, and later by Adam Smith and John Stewart Mill. Liberalism embodied the idea of protecting individual rights.

Radicalism was also an important concept because it raised the issue of equality. It was best defined by Rousseau. During the French Revolution, the enemy of radicalism was privilege.

To me, conservatism begins with England's Edmund Burke. He defended society against arbitrary power. Conservatism respected family, local community, and social class. Yet it protected freedom of thought. It cared about the individual and his rights.

While the blend of those ideas may have influenced Jefferson and others, they have been lost in modern times. The distinctions between them have not only been blurred, they have drastically changed. They were the ideals by which our nation was built, and the Republic of Texas created.

Lincoln often quoted Jefferson, and even though Jefferson founded the Democractic Party and Lincoln the Republican, their concerns for individual rights and limited government were similar. One of my favorite quotations attributed to Lincoln offers insight into how government should function. It helps explain what made this country successful and illustrates the effect of Lincoln's attitude upon government in the late 19th century. It is a philosophy that Texans have long understood and still support:

> "You cannot bring about prosperity by discouraging thrift. You cannot strengthen the weak by weakening the strong. You cannot help the wage earner by pulling down the wage payer. You cannot further the brotherhood of many by encouraging class hatred. You cannot help the poor by destroying the rich. You cannot establish sound security on borrowed money. You cannot keep out of trouble by spending more than you earn. You cannot build character and courage by taking away man's initiative and independence. You cannot help men permanently by doing for them what they could and should do for themselves."

Those are thoughts worth remembering—truths I have asked my children to memorize and understand.

Ideas are like hurricanes. Though often unseen they have tremendous power to build or destroy the national will and affect a country's character and destiny. Ideas can create and change nations, as well as local communities. Progress shifts back and forth between these two styles of politics: the organizational method of tactics and the philosophical magnetism of ideas.

We have reached this century with philosophies, values, and concerns that have been built and passed from generation to generation. These values lifted our forefathers to heights of achievement, because they believed in them sincerely. They had faith and goals that they were willing to die for. That is what we need today and for the difficult period ahead, if we are to rekindle the American Dream as it has been in the past.

"On a group of theories one can found a school, but on a group of values one can found a culture, a civilization, a new way of living together among men."

—IGNAZIO SILONE

V.

LEVELS OF AWARENESS

When our youngest daughter Elizabeth, affectionately known as Buffy, was four, she became infatuated with a doll she had seen advertised on television. On our way to a family vacation in Acapulco, we were fortunate enough to find one for her, and she treasured it dearly. I felt particularly content because I had acquired the doll that pacified her interest for the long trip. Once past immigration in the Acapulco airport, we entered the cavernous concrete customs terminal where the baggage circulated on a long, winding conveyor. As usual, the kids waited for me to get the baggage, with Buffy clasping her doll. Suddenly, the entire area echoed with her screams. Petrified, I thought she had been injured and rushed over to her. She was crying and pointing to the opposite side of the luggage conveyor where a man was holding her doll. He threw the doll back to me, and I gave it to her at which she screamed even louder. Discretion being the better part of valor, I took her to Kitty and rounded up the rest of the luggage.

Once in the customs section, I was relieved to see that Buffy was calmer. The customs official slowly examined each piece of luggage and slid it down a silver ramp as he completed it. During all of this, Buffy kept trying to put her doll on the table. The officer told her it wasn't necessary. To my surprise she began to cry again!

When we were finally in the taxi and headed to the hotel, I looked at Buffy, normally a very sweet-mannered child and asked her what was wrong. Her reply startled me: "Daddy, they were very mean men. They wouldn't let my doll ride the merry-go-round or ride the slide either. It's no fun there."

That is, perhaps, the best example I have ever run across of the different levels of understanding which can exist at the same time among different people regarding the same circumstance. Each of us looks at life's situations with dissimilar degrees of understanding. Parables are used in the Bible to teach lessons. When Christ was teaching, He used these stories for the general population. When He was alone with His disciples, He explained the stories' deeper meaning and symbolism.

Life itself can be perceived with varying depths of awareness. To understand the future, it becomes very important to have a broadened and knowledgeable perspective. Then we must bring those areas of awareness together in order to understand the reality of circumstances, and from that vantage point we can accomplish the best possible results.

One of the problems in reaching greater awareness is handling the constant flow of information from the media. America is pressured by accelerating change and increasing knowledge. Like a penny that is compounded 100% daily, the constant doubling amounts to millions of dollars in a month. The rate of growth of knowledge doesn't have to increase because the base is increasing so significantly. Effectively utilizing this information is the challenge.

In order to manage change, we are required to rely on our wisdom—which doesn't always grow as rapidly as new information. Modern man is infinitely more knowledgeable than his ancient predecessors. Each of us probably knows more about the workings of the human body than did the father of medicine, Hippocrates. An astronomy hobbyist probably knows more about the universe than did Copernicus. There is no evidence, however, that we are wiser than Solomon or Socrates. While our information grows, our wisdom, or ethics, does not always keep equal pace. In addition to deepening our knowledge in science, we need to expand knowledge in economics, geography, arts, and literature. The knowledge which these often provide is the material from which wisdom and breadth of perspective are distilled. Wisdom cannot be taught, but the breadth of knowledge and perspective on which it is based most assuredly can be. That is why tyrants are so careful about the contents of books. Their objective is not to cultivate true wisdom in their constituents since wisdom leads to analysis of ideas which are the foundations of politics, economics, and power. The family has an opportunity to establish values in children.

It is truly the base upon which commitment rests. The media provides us great amounts of increased information, but we have to look carefully at how that knowledge falls into categories and how it can be properly used if we are to acquire wisdom. Wisdom often requires a purpose and a vision of a much wider world and the interrelationships therein. Art can take us into a deeper appreciation of the world, such as Picasso's "Bull's Head" in which bicycle handlebars are combined with a seat to look like the head of a bull. It wasn't the object that was appreciated, but the creativity involved in putting those two pieces together to create something totally different from the two individual pieces. Art can provide different perspectives and ideas—and ideas are the essence of life.

Democracy, a free press, and freedom in the arts to express thought are interrelated. Many people feel that they have little control over their joint destiny with others as a nation, but in reality, it is each individual's decision, as it is swayed by politics, that sets our destiny. That right to vote carries a responsibility, not just to vote, but to judge carefully, and a responsibility to know the facts. To vote simply on the basis of a television commercial does not do it full justice. A realistic view requires taking the time to learn as much as possible and seeking the opinions of those you trust and respect. Difficult questions face us, but wisdom exists in a style of government that tries to coordinate many of these thoughts. By the nature of our economic problems, people will focus on candidates and issues. The important thing is that they not do so on emotion, but on thought and wisdom that can establish a proper trend and direction. If they have confidence in a vision and maintain a sense of morality and belief in God, people will have the strength and moral fiber to sacrifice, and our direction as a nation can be inherently more positive.

Both Texas and the United States face difficult challenges in these next several years. Natural resources will no longer carry the state forward; the national debt and international competition will necessitate difficult decisions nationally. Discussions on the issues facing us are taking place throughout the nation. However, people are perceiving those issues with different levels of understanding and awareness—just as Buffy and I had during our experience in Acapulco. Senator Phil Gramm pointed out to me that it is not the balancing of the budget that is the *real issue*, but rather it is the relationship of government with society. *What should the government be doing and what can it realistically hope to do?* We in America have lived through some of the most prosperous periods any nation has enjoyed. Margins in economics and military strength have let us adopt policies that bred complacency. But now, the margins have shrunk considerably, and we have a responsibility to establish the basics for an intelligent government. Our present standard of living allows us the conscious understanding to put forth new programs and new ideas to adjust to the changing times. But we will need statesmen rather than politicians to implement competent government.

In describing the differences between a statesman and a politician, James Freeman Clark said:

> "A politician looks at the next election and a statesman looks at the next generation.
>
> A politician looks to his party while a statesman looks to the nation.
>
> A politician is content to ride with the tide while the statesman tends to steer the boat."

If you were raised in a politically active family, you probably had a chance to see politics close up. You learned that it's a strange world of deal-making and compromising filled with professional politicians—whose concern, above all else—is to remain elected, as well as with people who are wishing to sacrifice themselves at the altar of political defeat for a noble cause, and with elected officials who try to practice statesmanship as much as their constituency will allow.

With all three groups, one thing is common. If the correct idea is popular, it has an excellent chance of success. Thus, selling ideas people can support is crucial. To understand the complex issues of today, however, we must raise people's level of awareness of those issues which are key to a positive direction for America.

We also need to elect people who are willing to take a stand and lead the public rather than follow it. Clues about a candidate's real nature are easily recognized once we know what to look for. It becomes a game of reading between the lines as we watch political advertisements or listen to random comments to the press. A smiling face and glib talk don't prove that a person can solve the tough problems of governing. Many people are far better at campaigning and marketing themselves through the media than they are at governing. To me, they are as superficial as their image on the television screen. They do real damage to Texas and the rest of the country, because their lack of leadership means we haven't used our potential for solving problems. Appointments too often are political, and the bureaucracy is untested.

Unfortunately, many candidates and office holders don't have many personal goals or ideas. They are more like a composite of the nation's changing opinions. They poll the country's mood every week or month, or as often as their pocketbooks allow, in order to find out how people feel about issues. Then they make public pronouncements in support of those issues, so that they can ride with the tide of public sentiment and emotion.

In judging a candidate, you need to look at two things—his personal abilities such as intelligence, vision, communication skills, and leadership strength, and then his motivation for wanting the office. What matters is not what he wants to be, but what he wants to do. The candidate's abilities need to be judged at a deeper level—can he understand all the issues and how they relate to each other? If he approaches issues individually, rather than looking to combine them all into a coordinated approach, he is probably political rather than visionary. The appointments he makes and the advisors he chooses can reveal how his mind works and what his purposes may be. Are the appointees knowledgeable, do they have the overview, do they have reputations for integrity and for getting things accomplished? Thus the candidate's style is very important. The scientific method with its five steps from hypothesis to conclusion may seem out of place in politics and government. But if a person's mind doesn't work logically and with purpose, he will never direct policy but will be directed by what issues surface. A leader must be able to distinguish mountains from molehills—or have the ability to select people to help him do so. Some of the best people in government do not know all the answers but know who to ask. They recognize two types of genius—very specialized such as the knowledge possessed by a physicist, or very broad, such as required to blend and orchestrate wide-ranging thoughts. A genius in one area is not necessarily gifted in the other. A good leader selects, or has selected for him, the right combination of appointees for the particular purpose. All of this demonstrates a person's leadership style, not his persuasive abilities, which are less important in the long run.

In many elections we see both sides emphasize the opposition's failings on single issues that may be important, but are certainly not as important as the overall direction of the state or nation. They illustrate what former British Prime Minister Disraeli meant when he said, "It is far easier to be critical than to be correct." In campaigns we listen to candidates promise far more than they can deliver. Meanwhile, the public continues demanding promises rather than an accounting of how candidates will implement the promises they or their party have already made.

When we start to judge government and politicians, we need first to have a clear idea of what role we expect government to play in our society. Then we can determine whether an individual is serving our interests or his own. In my viewpoint, a politician is someone who basically serves his own ego. A statesman is interested in serving the people. Very often a candidate can go in either direction depending upon the feedback he receives from his constituency. Most of us would rather have statesmen lead us than politicians—as long as the statesmen serve our personal interests. I believe that in the long run society will sustain itself, if we will agree that our personal interests are best served when government policies and laws protect the common good.

A statesman approaches issues and state affairs with all the wisdom and skill he possesses. His concern is for society as a whole, and he takes great personal pride in improving the quality of life for himself and others. A statesman is not a perfect human being. But he does tend to have certain hallmarks of maturity. His character is distinguished by a sense of personal and professional integrity. Through experience and a broadened perspective, he usually is able to discern the correct course of action for his state and nation. And he will govern his own life by a well-defined personal sense of virtue and principle. He understands the importance of morality. If we look to the long-term benefits provided by statesmen, we will not want to suffer politicians. But if our philosophy is to live for today and care nothing about others, then a politician will serve just fine, because he specializes in the quick-fix and the soothing rhetoric of concern.

Judging whether a candidate is a politician or a statesman is challenging. If the idea of statesmanship catches on, every politician will be one, and Madison Avenue will clone them by the hundreds. We will vote for statesmen who serve our personal interests and quickly retire those who care most about the common good. However, it defeats the purpose of carefully examining a candidate's views and motives if we fall prey to what is essentially just another game of salesmanship. We must be able to know a statesman when we see, hear, or read about one. Someone said that God gives every generation the leaders to make that generation great if we will listen to them. We are the people who can create an atmosphere in which statesmanship is allowed to function.

Dad taught you should judge a man by his heart and mind, not by his handshake and smile. That was his way of evaluating potential statesmen and potential politicians. Dad's advice is just as valid today as it was then. Maybe it's even more important now, since we tend to be further removed from a candidate. Few of us know him personally. We may meet briefly during a reception or dinner, shake hands, and the candidate smiles warmly. Yet we only get a superficial impression of the person. He may be extremely persuasive and charismatic, and people may vote for him based on that one meeting. But important questions often go unanswered. Is he just? Is he motivated to bring the state or nation together, or is he preoccupied with establishing political power and control?

Motivation is critically important in assessing the candidate as a leader, as well as in understanding his vision for the state or nation.

The people surrounding a statesman are as important as the candidate himself. They may become staff members if he wins the election, and their philosophies will also influence government. After discerning whether a candidate has the qualities of a statesman, party loyalty becomes important. However, this holds true only if the party remains consistent with its label and supports the principles of a free society.

Leaders have certain identifiable characteristics. They attempt to guide, not threaten, people. It is always better to unify than to divide. As Dad noted, the difference between force and inspiration is like the difference between night and day. Napoleon concluded that a great leader was a man "with velvet gloves on iron fists." In modern politics, there is a critical need for strength blended with diplomacy. Aggressive use of force reveals not only a problem of pride, but one of weakness and ignorance. It shows an inability to recognize how much the abuse of power actually costs—to others and to the leader himself.

A leader needs a sense of timing, excellent information sources, and advisors. They will help develop his strategy, allowing him to enter politics on the economic upturn and get out before the downturn. The leader will be at the heart of a movement. He will feel the heat of opposition and suffer the grinding of the political process. If you believe in certain principles and know what you want to see accomplished, it is vital that you choose a leader very wisely, because his abilities will have a great effect on how well the movement succeeds. He has to understand that policy which coordinates change begins at the highest levels of government, and the responsibility for constructive change belongs to him.

A number of leaders come to mind when I think of statesmen. These men may not have been correct all the time, and undoubtedly had personality flaws as all of us do. But on the whole they had the best interests of all people in mind when they considered public issues. They looked beyond their own comfort zone and took risks for the betterment of society as they perceived it. They advanced noble ideals as much as possible. Conscience triumphed over convenience.

When I think about American statesmen, Thomas Jefferson and Abraham Lincoln come instantly to my mind. In Texas, I think that Governors Allan Shivers and John Connally exhibited hallmarks of statesmanship. They addressed major issues such as education and concerned themselves with what could be prepared for future generations. Former Attorney General and Secretary of State John Ben Shepherd, who spent a lifetime serving on commissions to promote the cultural arts as well as business, greatly contributed to the future of Texas and is a statesman.

All of these men I have mentioned have something in common—they cared less for honors than the good accomplished, and they recognized the importance of ideas. For example, Jefferson could have placed upon his tombstone that he was President, that he had made the Louisiana Purchase and expanded American territory and that he was an achiever in many fields. However, he did not pride himself on these accomplishments. Instead, he was an excellent example of someone who kept an eye on the future while he grappled with the everyday problems of the early colonies and a new nation. His tombstone inscription read,

> "Here was buried Thomas Jefferson author of
> the Declaration of Independence, of the
> Statutes of Virginia for religious freedom,
> and father of the University of Virginia."

Ideas are enduring, and if we wish to affect the world, we have to understand how to change and move toward the great ideals and theories which can provide solutions. If we do not have a port toward which we are steering, we will drift at sea. Great men make a difference in life, but they are not nearly as important as the ideas they espouse. Confucius occupied a position similar to a city manager in Lu province. He died without knowing that his ideas would be followed by billions of people one day. Buddha was a prince who became a monk in search of truth, and the concepts of life and relationships between people which he taught have changed the lives of huge populations. People support Christianity, Islam, and Judaism with tremendous intensity—ideas are the greatest legacy.

Perhaps it is best said in a quotation by him or an unknown author which was found in former Governor Shivers' briefcase shortly after his death and placed on his tombstone. It expressed the essence of what he, Dad, and a generation of men who possessed a deep level of understanding believed:

> "Fame is a vapor, popularity an
> accident, and riches take wing.
> Those who cheer today curse
> tomorrow,
> Only one thing remains—character."

Beyond concern for the common good and the desire to influence a state or nation positively, leadership style is important. Correctly judging a leader's style is critical, because it often tells you whether he can successfully command respect. People can be led in many ways. Some styles produce difficulty, while others encourage us toward achievement and excellence. A statesman wants to inspire people, while a politician hopes to lull them to sleep so they won't listen too closely. Strong leaders have confidence in their ideas, and they have an ability to inspire other people. Less successful leaders are more interested in maintaining short-term political superiority. They often use coalitions and political intimidation to accomplish their ends. Even though statesmanship is noble, not every candidate or leader will see it as desirable. Many candidates believe that the public is shallow and would not support them if they began voting for the common good instead of short-term interests. They insist that there's no room for principle or statesmanship in practical politics today. I do not agree. Their view is shortsighted. There are now, and always have been, both politicians and statesmen. It is a question of focus and whether the environment is conducive to a majority of one or the other. If statesmanship is not popular, what causes some people to embrace it at the risk of losing everything politically?

President John F. Kennedy explained the heart of that quality in his book, *Profiles in Courage:*

> "What then caused the statesmen to act as they did? It was not because they loved the public better than themselves. On the contrary, it was precisely because they did love themselves—because each one's need to maintain his own respect for himself was more important to him than his popularity with others—because his desire to win or maintain a reputation for integrity and courage was stronger than his desire to maintain his office—because his conscience, his personal will was stronger than the pressures of public disapproval—because his faith that his courage was the best one, and would ultimately be vindicated, outweighed his fear of public reprisal."

Perhaps nothing is more important to a statesman's viewpoint than strengthening and maintaining a nation's will. Ideas are needed to inspire that will. Morality is needed to provide the confidence that gives it character. Vision is needed to inspire sacrifice. A statesman understands the importance of partisanship, which involves ideas grouped together, but he also recognizes its limits.

Statesmanship and wisdom include the ability to listen to opposite views and admit that one does not have all the answers. Sound reason, not strict ideology, must be the basis for national and state leadership.

This will emerge, primarily in the field of economics, and later influence all other areas of our society.

I have received a great deal of criticism because I have been an independent through much of my life and have worked for both Democratic and Republican candidates at high levels. Often I am told that I must choose between one or the other, that ideas are either Republican or Democratic by who sponsored them. Unfortunately, ideas are better judged as good or bad, and often times the best ideas are blended in order to fit into the world's realities. Difficult economic choices loom in the future, and many of them are upon us now. A banker realizes two things about a loan, as Dad used to point out to me. The first is that all of the paper in the world doesn't make a good loan if the man can't repay the loan. Reality eventually triumphs over appearance. The second is that we are all in this world together. The ripple effect in our economy makes the benefit or the pain felt by one in part shared by all. As a result, we need philosophies that are not Democratic or Republican, but are American and supported in a bipartisan manner. It is often said this is not possible in today's political world. I am told political overtones dominate everything in Austin and Washington. But that is not necessarily the proper viewpoint. Both the Democratic and Republican parties, I feel, have the same long-term objectives, a strong, prosperous, and free nation. I think they differ, however in the approaches to the problems that confront us. I perceive the Republican party as believing strongly in the moral superiority of free enterprise as an instrument for achieving the highest standards of living and as a guarantor of individual freedoms. It recognizes that the benefits of free enterprise are not distributed equally and do not erase all instances of social injustice, but it fears that state-sponsored initiatives which go too far in addressing these problems are likely to threaten the vitality of the free enterprise system and result in net losses for society as a whole.

I also perceive that the Democratic party seeks a strong and viable free enterprise system. However, it holds government responsible for ameliorating economic inequities in order to preserve a political and social climate in which free enterprise can be sustained. Neither party has a monopoly on wisdom or on nobility of ultimate objectives. The Republican party is not, as overzealous Democratic partisans would have us believe, a party of fat cats and special interests. Nor is the Democratic party, as overzealous Republicans would have us believe, a party of meddlers and collectivists. The American society has succeeded because there has been a balance of views. A strong support for the economic system is essential if we are not to become so obsessed with social and economic inequities that we forget that the free enterprise system, which has been the ultimate source of our prosperity and our freedoms, requires constant attention to the economic incentives which have made us what we are. A strong concern for the common man is essential if we are not to become so obsessed with the pure ideology of our economic policies that we forget the needs of the people whose voices are required to sustain them.

History suggests that these ideas played out by both parties are critically important to a free and sustainable society. Had the philosophy of caring for social and economic inequities been introduced into the Roman Empire, its collapse might have been reversed. Roman rulers may have been more attentive to the plight of the masses who were driven to lawlessness by the economic decline. Similarly, had a strong free enterprise system been introduced into Czarist Russia, it would have assisted in breaking down feudal barriers and smoothing the transition to the industrial revolution. Concentration of wealth in a small minority would have been eliminated, thus destroying the fertile ground from which the Bolshevik Revolution sprang.

The future, thus, of our families may rest on our choice of economic systems for the future, but it also rests with the political philosophies we adopt to enhance that system. If our political system is to rise above partisanship and find an American philosophy it will only do so because we as Americans demand it. Like our economic system, it reacts to us. The key issues will be discussed because reality will bring them to the forefront. They will get more attention because they affect our individual pocketbooks and our way of life. The best way each of us can guarantee that the right policies are chosen is to take individual responsibility to learn what we feel are the right answers. Then, it is important to convey those studied opinions to our Congressmen, whom we choose not on the basis of what they want to be, but what they want to do, and to family, friends, and the general public. In this way, we can focus attention on the most critical issues, thereby contributing toward positive change which will rebuild America's competitiveness and leave a legacy of economic growth to our children.

A statesman will support his party, but he also appreciates the need for cooperation between parties when the national interest is at stake. Good government is good politics. A statesman usually emerges during times of crisis and peril as a response to the citizens' push for action. Crisis calls for vision—not partisanship—and it is the genius of a statesman which allows him to rise above politics to seek the best for his country.

In discerning whether a candidate or office holder tries to practice statesmanship, it is important to determine where he wants to take the government. Every candidate should be required to answer that question before he solicits a vote from us. Too often, a candidate briefly listens to a conversation, and five minutes later he repeats what he thinks the voter wants to hear. He probably has little overall understanding of government's powers and what the role of government should be. His basic concerns center on how he will be listed in the history books and whether he will be treated as an elder statesman at cocktail parties in his old age. Or he might simply hope that he can manipulate the media and photo sessions well enough to last through his term in office and retire in dignity.

That is not the thinking of a statesman. Without the goal to improve government, a person would be better off working behind the scenes or in another profession which could help society. If someone wants to be involved in government, he or she needs to affirm definite principles and purpose.

Today, there are political leaders who want to be statesman, but fear that their constituents would not re-elect them to office. They think that voting on principle is political suicide. Many times they are right. We all share responsibility for their concern. If we would encourage our leaders to exercise statesmanship, then we must make a commitment to support them when tough decisions arise. Even when we are affected negatively, we must have the maturity to realize that we ultimately benefit by supporting the common good. Statesmanship implies risk-taking, and some decisions may not produce successful results. Other strategies may require several years to bear fruit. We must be willing to demonstrate patience and wait out the difficult years, until the government or economy has had time to adjust. If we see ourselves as governing partners with our representatives, then we will ride out the bad decisions as well as enjoy the good ones. We will take equal responsibility with them. In a sense, then, all of us will be practicing the high art of statesmanship.

We will stand in agreement with John F. Kennedy when he said:

". . . . in a democracy, every citizen, regardless of his interest in politics, holds office . . . We the people are the boss, and we will get the kind of political leadership, be it good or bad, that we demand and deserve."

"True democracy, living and growing and inspiring, puts its faith in the

people—faith that the people will not simply elect men who will represent their views ably and faithfully, but also elect men who will exercise their conscientious judgement—faith that the people will not con-
demn those whose devotion to principle leads them to unpopular
courses, but will reward courage, respect honor, and ultimately recognize right."

It is one thing to recognize problems and another to correct them.
Today's world is very complex, and the task of building a coordinated philosophy is difficult. To accomplish this, we must rise above normal understanding and grasp for a higher awareness that puts the world and its
problems in a new perspective. But it is necessary that we bring all our
people to this level, for the people as a whole, by their action or inaction,
determine the nation's destiny far more than their leaders. Leaders inspire us with ideas, but the people must react. It is easy to become discouraged with the apathy abounding today, but we must remember that
crisis and fear generate intensified focus on ideas. Questions about our
economic future, and awareness of the pressures facing Texas now, are
strengthening our concern.

Pressure focuses attention, and we are to the point that effective
ideas put forth by the right type of leaders can generate power. A consensus can be built among people who may be in different parties but have
the same principles and ideas. A set of coordinated principles based on
ideas is important to any governmental style. We must be careful, however, that in building this set of principles that may form a style of government, we do not mold it into an inflexible ideology that cannot adjust to
changing situations.

Even with a structure of guiding ideas, however, we need to remain
open-minded. For example, statesmanship requires understanding the
opposition's arguments and judging their merits objectively. Blind adherence to one's own beliefs, without being open to refining and adapting
them to changing times, does them an injustice. There will always be opposing extremities of political thought, but I personally do not believe that
the modern world will allow us to find answers to our social and economic
problems in ideological purity.

If statesmen are expected to exercise wisdom, then all Americans
need a strong national will which includes the ability to listen to dissenting
views, admit we don't have final answers, and agree that sound reason,
not strict ideology, must set the basis for state and national leadership. I
don't mean to imply, however, that a person shouldn't have a strong set of

principles which he tries to communicate to others. I mean that we have to work together to build a national, bipartisan consensus. That requires a willingness to communicate and to seek the best answers.

Discussions between liberals and conservatives can provide a broadened perspective on issues. Perhaps we believe life would be better if everything was settled and certain—but that would be boring. Strife is part of our human experience, and politics is simply the crucible where pressures can be settled.

In summary, Texas' style of government must reflect that times will change, and we may have to establish principles of government that could be categorized as ideologies. However, allegiance should not be paid to an established set of ideas just because they may be traditional, but rather to those ideas which provide the best government for the people.

Whatever ideology we choose to follow in Texas, some of our most important questions will be based upon what we perceive to be the purpose of our lives and the type of legacy we want to pass on to the next generation.

A while ago, a friend shared with me Rabbi Robert I. Kahn's book, *Lessons for Life*. In the book, Kahn told the true story of Rabbi Akavia who lived almost 2000 years ago. The Rabbi instructed his followers to "reflect upon three things and you will not succumb to sin: whence you came, whither you are bound, and before Whom you must give account." Before reading that book, I had been taught that I should do my duty to God, country, and myself. But the Rabbi's comments seemed to speak such a simple truth. What we do with the time between when we are born and die is our own responsibility, and someday we shall be called to account.

We now have a prime opportunity to set the course of our state and nation. What has been called the "spirit" of Texas can lead this state and the rest of America through the tangled undergrowth of difficult problems into a better day. That famous Texas spirit was the driving force behind the men and women who sacrificed their lives at the Alamo. It was also a legacy of concern for the common good. Texas' greatest influence in Washington came not from the power of men but from the power of that idea. Texans have been for the country, not just a state, and that gave them power in Washington. It was best said by House Speaker Sam Rayburn in his maiden Congressional speech on May 6, 1913, and which promise he followed for 48 years:

> "It is now my sole purpose here to help enact such wise and just laws that our *common country* will by virtue of these laws be a happier and a

more prosperous country. I have always dreamed of a country which I
believe this should be and that is one in which the citizenship is an educated and patriotic people, not swayed by passion and prejudice and a
country that shall know no east, no west, no north, no south, but in-
habited by a people liberty loving, patriotic, happy and prosperous,
with its lawmakers having no other purpose than to write such just
laws that shall in the years to come be of service to humankind yet
unborn."

It is that same strength of character which can lead our state and the
nation onto firmer ground. Perhaps some people look at Texans as boast-
ful, uncultured or behind-the-times. I have always viewed these same
traits differently. I believe that what sounds like boasting is just how we
express our deep affection and appreciation for Texas and everything that
it stands for. It is pride, not in the sense of vanity, but in the sense of
respect. The way we express ourselves is an outgrowth of the Texas
landscape itself. If you have ever climbed through the mountains of the
Big Bend country in 100 degree heat with the sun beating upon you and
the only available shade was under rocks where rattlers have already set
up residence, then you begin to understand what makes the bold Texas
spirit. That gusto comes from testing your heart, mind, and body against
the elements. Part of the land is untamed, and so is a part of the Texan
spirit. It is unfortunate that the image of Texas is too often portrayed on
television as a cow-country culture or a state populated by fast-moving,
slick-talking oilmen. That is not the Texas that I have known.

Most Texans have a profound sense of honor. During a football game
that I recall, one of the ends blocked a defensive back on a sweep. He hit
him extremely hard and damaged his knee. Obviously everyone regretted
the injury. But observers had to decide whether it was an accident or a
purposeful act. If it happened simply because the end was doing the best
possible job he could do and hitting as hard as he could, then he was to be
respected and not faulted. If, on the other hand, it was a cheap shot, he
would be held in extremely low regard. The point is that Texas has a tradition few people realize. We expect everyone to play tough, but not
mean. The same is true in its politics. You are expected to win and do the
very best you can, because that is the level at which you are judged.
People note how well you use your capacity. But cheating, cheap shots, or
mean character will not be tolerated. It is part of the Texas tradition of
honor. During his passive revolution in India, Mahatma Gandhi strongly
believed that if you are to win, you had to win in the right way and for the
right reasons. Texas is not passive. It is active. But it believes in the
same code of justice and honor.

Another part of our common legacy is a solid belief that encompasses limited government, individual freedom to achieve one's greatest potential, strong faith in God's unchanging principles, and the sanctity of the home, adherence to conservative economics, self-government by a citizenry educated in all these principles, and a healthy respect for the importance of every human being. Those ideas, coupled with confidence and abiding faith, are the bedrock of our belief structure and can be the foundation of a positive and realistic style of government in the future, one that looks less at partisanship and more at common sense and long-range vision. Texans realize that solutions should not be labeled as Democratic or Republican, but as good or bad. We must force our political system to think along these lines by allocating our support accordingly.

Idealism is a component of our legacy also. We are all a part of an American dream of freedom and independence, but perhaps Texans are more vocal about these principles. Sometimes newcomers seem a little embarrassed when we start talking about these ideals. It is not that they don't agree, it is just that it is not sophisticated to talk like that in New York or Washington, D.C. Fortunately, we can still talk openly about these values to others. We teach them to our children, and sometimes you might catch a few tears in our eyes when we do.

We are bringing with us the values of life that made this state and country great. Spiritual life is important to Texans, and it is part of a legacy which is imperative to our success as a state and nation. It is a private matter to most of us, but deeply felt. It forms the moral code that ties together the rest of the Texan character. Texans have never felt it was a sign of weakness to be sentimental over their devotion to God. A number of leading Texas businesspeople and politicians have expressed their belief that the will of Texas must be aligned with the will of God, if we hope to prosper as a society. It is more than just religious observances, however. It is adherence to a moral code that not only unifies people, but gives us a purpose to life and a satisfaction of accomplishment. It builds our will and motivates us to seek a greater destiny.

As Christ told His followers, as recorded in Matthew, Chapter 5: ". . . Love your enemies, and pray for those who persecute you . . . for if you love those who love you, what reward have you? Do not even the tax-gatherers do the same? And if you greet your brothers only, what do you do more than others?" This is a key point which is often forgotten. You have an obligation to affirmatively do the right thing, and the level of consciousness necessary to recognize one's duty is higher than we often encounter in our day-to-day activities where our emotions control us.

In this same spirit, the great statesmen among us will be those who are willing to extend their hands in friendship and trust to others who are also trying to build a more unified society. America is the one nation that can still lead the world. We held that position of leadership in industrial capacity and military might after World War II. We helped the rest of the world rebuild, and they became major competitors who now challenge us. When we were in a stronger position in the world, we often used our power to help others. Yet we did so when we could have dominated them because of our moral principles and values. Much of the world now condemns America. We receive little support from our few allies other than England. We could react negatively, but it is more important that we try to understand the economic consequences of their reliance upon oil from the Mideast and the indecision and stagnation that has taken place in Europe over these past years.

When Texas celebrated the Sesquicentennial in 1986, there were celebrations at the Alamo, San Jacinto, and the Texas capitol. The national media portrayed the festivities as Texas having a party while the price of oil was going downhill. It was predicted that the state would soon be in a position of economic decline. Some said Texas would not grow industrially, because she would have to increase taxes. God had helped Texas by putting oil beneath her soil. Now Texans were going to suffer the same problems as the rest of the country.

Texans viewed the Sesquicentennial from a different perspective. The people who chose to stay at the Alamo did so with the full knowledge of the consequences. Tremendously outnumbered, and at the end without hope of replacements, they could have fled, but they, like others in history, felt allegiance to duty, a conviction and a purpose. In the face of such odds, the military strategy is questionable, but it was a dramatic commitment. That commitment itself changed the entire course of the war by buying time for Sam Houston. After the battle was over, Santa Anna uniquely contributed to his own defeat. He ordered the bodies of the Texans piled up and burned as a symbol of what would happen to all who stood against him. Some like to believe that the smoke from those funeral pyres spread all over Texas and fell onto the soil, enriching it with a spirit of liberty and determination found nowhere else. It was certainly evident at the battle of San Jacinto, and it seems to have been a critical force in molding the state.

The question now is whether we can recapture this determination and reaffirm those strong values of family and individual responsibility. We must determine if we can make the sacrifices necessary to advance us toward greater destiny. Can we create a third coast of thought and weave ideas into the national fabric? It is important to remember that what can be accomplished always falls somewhere on a line between what we desire and what is realistic. The element that can locate that point is our will to achieve. The change starts with an individual; it starts in families, communities and neighborhoods; and it begins with people taking a stand. The more dedicated and committed we are, the more intelligently we choose our policies, the greater the opportunity for a better destiny for our children.

Putting our economic and political houses in order will require sacrifice by the state and nation. But perhaps that can be achieved by a growing understanding of what wisdom in government can provide. We have to raise our children to understand those same principles and processes—not in terms of how they can selfishly benefit from them, but rather how they are obligated to make a contribution. Deepening awareness involves much more than political issues. It means developing a clear understanding of life and the purposes for living—family, society, and God.

DEDICATION

A dedication often accompanies the prologue to a book, but somehow this seemed more meaningful as a conclusion. One's life and character are forever changed and affected by many people. Relationships, whether brief or extended, create a dynamic existence. Family and friends, not material wealth, are the treasures of life. They are the secrets to happiness. A primary orientation to them and to God sets one on a path that allows material success. But at some time in his life, a person must make a decision to stand for what he believes against tough odds. He becomes committed to his convictions or conscience, abandoning the safety of convenience. As a whole, this is true of a nation of individuals.

Thus this book is properly dedicated to parents, family, and friends who are dear on a personal basis, as well as to the ideals they hold. Each has contributed so much to my life and to the development of ideas which have been my mainstay. Therefore, this book is dedicated also to those ideas.

Those ideas have been given expression by an organization—the Texas Lyceum. The name "Lyceum" is a tribute to Aristotle, since it describes the place where he taught. It represents the spirit of sharing concerns of common interest, integrity, and intelligent vision. The Lyceum was formed in 1980 to attract younger generation leaders from all political parties, social groups and perspectives. Many individuals and organizations worked to make the Lyceum a reality, and I want to express my appreciation for their efforts. A group of 45 young leaders and an advisory group of the state's senior leadership developed a concept of bringing people together from Texas' vast regions, so that they might get acquainted, understand each other's viewpoints, and build awareness which could later be used in meeting the state's challenges. *Texas Business* magazine helped invite the statewide media. Dr. George Kozmetsky and the Institute of Constructive Capitalism coordinated the academic and research institutions.

Over the years, the Texas Lyceum has invited numerous speakers from throughout the world and nation to discuss concerns and ideas with Texans. The organization prioritizes what issues are important to the state's future, looks at the component parts of what affects us, and ana-

lyzes how they relate to each other. It organizes "think tanks" to research independent issues and then offers forums for analyzing opposing
viewpoints in order to refine key concepts and ideas for presentations to
decision-makers through its publication entitled *The Lyceum Journal.*

However, the Lyceum's finest characteristic is that it brings out the
best in people. Dad used to say that people are seldom against you; they
are normally for themselves. By studying issues, we have found that the
common good can regulate policy and bring unexpected unity. One friend
said that the Lyceum stood for the highest ideals in Texas and the country, because it tried to bring people together with integrity. The organization elevated the state and nation above politics, and that mixture provided a catalyst for visionary change, because it could build consensus
and support for overall governmental goals. It blended respect for the
wisdom of age and tradition with the enthusiasm and ingenuity of youth to
set a base for intelligent change.

Thus it is appropriate to dedicate this book as well to the Lyceum's
ideals and to the group that volunteered their names for that first great
endeavor, as well as all the subsequent members, friends, and other organizations that have arisen from ideas generated as a result of Lyceum
friendships.

Six ravens with clipped wings stay at the Tower of London, because
a legend of many centuries warns that the monarchy will fall if they leave.
Similarly, the Lyceum is to me such a symbol for Texas' future. It stands
for the embodiment of character: honor, loyalty to the state, dedication to
a cause, and clarity of vision. And as we have seen in this book, character
will be our destiny.